Goal Achievement

through

Treasure Mapping

Not knowing when the dawn will come,
I open every door.

Emily Dickinson

Goal Achievement

through

Treasure Mapping

A Guide to Personal and Professional Fulfillment

Barbara Laporte, M.A.

HeartLifter Publications
St. Paul

Copyright © 2005 by Barbara J. Laporte
All rights reserved. No part of this publication may be
reproduced, distributed, or transmitted in any form or by
any means, including photocopying, recording, or other
electronic or mechanical methods, without the prior written permission of the author, except in the case of brief
quotations embodied in critical reviews and certain other
noncommercial uses permitted by copyright law. For permission requests, write to:

HeartLifter Publications
P.O. Box 18453
Minneapolis, MN 55418

The author appreciates the permission granted from
Anthony Robbins and Simon & Schuster to use the material from *Unlimited Power*.

To learn more about Barbara's consulting services, please
visit: www.laportecareerconsulting.com or email her at
Barb@laportecareerconsulting.com

This book is dedicated
to the memory of Phil Laporte,
an angel in heaven,
whose teachings live on in the hearts of so many;
and to
Brad Loken and Becca Loken—my loving children,
Dream-Seekers extraordinaire!

Contents

Acknowledgments

Where do I begin? So many people have blessed my path to this book. In order of appearance, as it were, I appreciate my friend Mel Robinson's encouragement to apply for the job that led me to Terri O'Grady, who recommended the Catherine Ponder books. Barbara Winter and John Schroeder were with me early on, each an inspirational role model. To the friends and clients who were willing to try treasure mapping and share their experiences, and especially those whose stories are told here, a most heartfelt thank you. To those who never knew that they had a role in encouraging me, I am grateful for the serendipity of your presence in my journey at the right time and place. To Richard Leider, willing to share his process and advice, thank you. To Donna Bennett, mentor, friend, and treasure mapping hostess beyond compare, my deepest thanks. To my dear DHS friends, Barb Bender, Lyn Turton, and Marilyn Wallick, who give friendship a whole new dimension, hugs to each of you. To Cindy Rogers, who provided gentle and professional editing, I can't tell you how much I appreciate you! Last, but not certainly not least, a huge thank you to my husband, Ron Lewandowski, who provides unfailing love and support—you are an angel on earth. How very blessed I am by your presence in my life.

Preface

Hold fast to dreams,
For if dreams die,
Life is a broken-winged bird
That cannot fly . . .

Langston Hughes

Re-Awaken Your Dream Seeker

Once upon a time there was a little girl. She was a happy child, full of wonder about the world, which to her was a magical, exciting place. One day, she was out for a walk with her mother and she saw a whole flock of birds soaring high in the sky.

"Look at the beautiful birds, Mommy!" she cried. "Someday I will fly like the birds do!"

Her mother, who was in something of a hurry, remarked, "You can't fly. You're a little girl, and everyone knows that little girls can't fly. Now come along." The child, still gazing at the birds, shrugged her shoulders and ran to catch up with her mother.

A few years later, as an elementary school student, the little girl became fascinated with all things having to do with the ocean. In particular, she loved learning about the dolphins and read about them every chance she got. As she sat in her classroom one afternoon, she read that there were places where people could go to actually swim with the dolphins. She jumped up and practically skipped to the teacher's desk, enthusiastically exclaiming, "Dolphins are wonderful! Someday I am going to go swimming with them!"

Her teacher reminded her, "Well, you are not a dolphin, you are a young lady, and young ladies do not swim with dolphins. Now get to back to your assignment." Her spirits dampened, the child reluctantly returned to her seat.

When she got to high school, her geography class watched videos about other countries. Her imagination soared, and the girl announced to her friends, "Someday, I will travel all over the world and visit every one of those countries!"

Her friends replied, "Like you're going to travel alone. Get real. No way could you ever do that." The girl fell silent, wondering if perhaps her friends were right. Maybe she was foolish to have such desires.

After that, she began keeping her dreams and wishes to herself, since sharing them with others usually led to discouraging responses. Eventually, she simply stopped dreaming altogether, for if she felt a glimmer of a dream starting, just as quickly she would hear little voices say, "You can't. You're not. No way."

What do you suppose became of this child?

Let me invite you to look into a mirror. No matter what your gender, if you have ever heard the little voices that say, "You can't, you're not, no way" and allowed them to kill one of your dreams, you will see the child of this story reflected there.

The good news is that the Dream-Seeker—the other part of that child who remains full of wonder about the world, who says, "I will!" and who believes in all of life's exciting possibilities—is still very much alive within each of us, too. The purpose of this book to reawaken the Dream-Seeker within you. Let your Dream-Seeker help you remember your goals and dreams, and let this book guide you on your journey to accomplish them. Using a goal achievement process called treasure mapping, you will learn how to attain personal and professional fulfillment, and once again realize the magic of your world!

Chapter 1

Choices

It is not our abilities that show us what we truly are.
It is our choices.

Professor Dumbledore in J.K. Rawlings'
Harry Potter and the Chamber of Secrets

Some people might say that I discovered the power of
treasure mapping by accident. I prefer to say I discovered
it by choice. At one of the lowest points in my life, I was
unemployed and newly divorced with sole custody of my
two small children. Out of work for almost ten months,
I was so discouraged I had even quit reading the want
ads to look for jobs. Fortunately for me, a friend of mine
who did read the paper happened to see a position adver-
tised that seemed like a good fit for my background and
experience. He encouraged me to apply for it. Reluctantly, I did. It was not that I didn't want to work, but

between my divorce and a series of job-search rejections, my self-esteem was already suffering. I didn't want to be rebuffed yet again, and it felt as though it was becoming more and more difficult to make a positive impression on prospective employers. So, it was with a fair amount of hesitation that I submitted my cover letter and resume' for the position my friend had seen.

Surprisingly, I was invited in for an interview, which went well enough that I was invited in for a second, during which I would need to make a presentation to five people. They told me they would make their selection based on the candidate's creativity, professionalism, knowledge of what the job entailed, and customization to the organization. This seemed a large order, and I began to doubt my ability to pull it off. With only a couple days to prepare, I felt increasing pressure to come up with something to meet their criteria. But trying to be creative seemed futile. One night, feeling particularly despondent, I climbed into bed and offered up something of a prayer, which I later realized was really more of an affirmation. It was something like, "If I am supposed to get this job, I will have a great idea." Oddly enough, in the middle of the night, I woke up with the idea for my presentation practically pouring out of me. It seemed so creative that I was actually excited to present it. The search committee liked it too, and I got the job.

Your only choice is what experiences you will
create.

Gary Zukav and Linda Francis

In my new position, I met a woman who introduced
me to a book by Catherine Ponder, called *Open Your
Mind to Receive.* It was there that I first read about
using "wheels of fortune" or picture collages to help
manifest what I want to have happen in my life. Shortly
after reading that book, I happened to read another
book called *Creative Visualization,* by Shakti Gawain.
She also wrote about using pictures to represent images
of goals and referred to this process as treasure mapping. After hearing about the same thing in a short time
period from more than one source, it began to occur to
me that perhaps the Universe was trying to tell me something. So, although the whole concept of pasting up pictures of my goals seemed almost too simple, I made the
choice to try it. Thus began my first treasure mapping
adventure.

My first treasure map was for a new marriage partner, but equally important, I wanted a male role model
for my four-year-old daughter and especially for my
son, who was seven years old. Having grown up with
an absentee father myself, I really wanted a husband
who would be there emotionally and physically while
the children were growing up. The treasure map was

incredibly simple: On pink construction paper, I glued a picture of a man and a woman who looked very much in love. I glued the words "forever love" right on top of the picture. Across the top of the paper, in pink magic marker, I wrote "Love, Harmony, Marriage, Happiness in Human Relationships." Interestingly, both of the books I had read mentioned the use of affirmations, and I remembered my simple affirmation before I got my job. This time, I was much more intentional about my affirmation, which I wrote at the bottom of the page:

> My right and perfect partner [and special friendships] will be mine
>
> in the right way, at the right time, through the right channels.
>
> I cooperate with the Divine Order in my life, and I am receiving now.

By placing the treasure map on the bulletin board in my bedroom, I saw it first thing every morning and right before I went to bed. The affirmation became like a mantra to me, and I would find myself saying it while I was showering, dressing, driving, washing dishes, and going to sleep.

In her book, Catherine Ponder discusses the power of release. She writes: "The act of release is one of the most effective ways to open your mind to receive. . . . It is available on the mental, emotional and physical planes. . . ."

In other words, if you have a particular goal that you wish to accomplish, you need to make room for it by releasing any mental or emotional blocks you may have about it. The same is true for physical objects. Here is the way this worked in my case:

Since my treasure map was for a new marriage partner, I realized I would need to identify and release whatever blocks I might have about love relationships. Even though the divorce had been my idea, I recognized that I still felt a certain amount of anger (an emotional block) towards my ex-husband. Through counseling, I was able to work through my feelings in order to get to a degree of understanding where I could honestly say that I wished him well. Around that time, I found a box of cards and love letters he had given me. There was a part of me that wanted to keep them—just to remind myself that if I never met anyone else, there had once been someone who had loved me. However, I came to realize that it was mostly fear (that there wouldn't be another relationship) that was motivating me to keep them. Thus, even these cards and letters could be a physical block to my ability to attract a new relationship. So one day, when I felt ready to release them without a sense of regret and without negative feelings towards my ex, I took each one and tore it in half. As I did this, I thought of my ex-husband and said, "I release you and let you go. You are free and I am free. I wish you well." (See chapter 4 for more about releasing, including activities you can do to help with the process.) All of the torn bits went into a plastic bag, which I tied up and took to the outside garbage can. The feeling of emancipation that came over me as I walked back to the house was amazing! It seemed as if the cards and letters had symbolized some sort of chain to the past; releasing them had released its hold on me, allowing me to now move freely into the future.

Meanwhile, I continued to visualize my new partner and say the affirmation I had written on my treasure map. A few months later, when the children and I attended a Thanksgiving Eve service at our church, the minister made a strange comment. He asked us to think of what it was in our lives that we were not particularly grateful for and to write it down as though we were thankful for it. "Yeah, right," I thought to myself. At that moment, my son and daughter were arguing over who got to hold the hymnal, so I wrote: "I am thankful for the opportunity to be a single mother." I didn't really feel that way, but the minister's point was that if we can be grateful for the circumstances of our lives that make us unhappy, perhaps we could start to see them differently. And as I thought about it, it did occur to me that having the opportunity to be a single mother gave me the chance to bond much more closely with my children than I might have otherwise.

The following Sunday, as I was leaving church, the

minister, whose name was Phil, mentioned that he wanted to borrow my kids sometime. Smiling, I said that would only work if he borrowed them for a month! Little did either of us know at the time, but he was going to "borrow" them for the rest of his life.

Phil called later in the week to see if the three of us would go to a Christmas concert with him that was geared for children. Naturally, I accepted. Who was I to refuse the minister? I anticipated a pleasant, perhaps somewhat self-conscious evening, so was rather unprepared for what actually happened. When we went on our "date," not only did we both thoroughly enjoy being with each other, but the chemistry between us was palpable. And equally important, he and the kids really liked each other! Five months and two days later, Phil and I got married.

Getting married to Phil was my first successful treasure mapping experience. And as it turned out, my desire for a marriage partner and role model for my children as they grew up was precisely what I received. The year that my son turned eighteen and my daughter fifteen, Phil died from stomach cancer. Despite this incredible loss, all three of us are grateful that we had the privilege of sharing a part of his life.

And remember that part of my treasure map affirmation was for "special friendships"? When Phil died, I went to a grief support group where I met three women who have become very special friends. The four of us were all in our forties when we lost our husbands, and this common bond added a dimension to our relationship that we would not experience otherwise. So, although my treasure map for a marriage partner turned out differently than I expected, I did manifest exactly what I intended: a male role model for my children as they were growing up and incredibly special friendships. This is why I believe intentionality is such an important part of treasure mapping.

To this day, I continue to use treasure mapping to manifest my goals. Once again, a treasure map for a partner has been successful, and I have been blessed with another wonderful man with whom to share my life. More successful treasure mapping experiences—my own as well as my clients—are described in the remaining chapters of this book.

I don't believe I discovered the power of treasure mapping by accident. We are constantly being offered choices about what we will do with our lives. Where those choices will take us, we can't always know. Remember the old adage that "when life hands you lemons make lemonade?" When I made the choices to apply for the job, read the books that were recommended, act on the suggestions from the books, and go to a grief support group, I had no idea what would unfold; but at some level, I was willing to "make lemonade." And I have no idea where my life journey would have taken me had I not made those choices. What I do know is this: In making the choices I did, I discovered treasure mapping—a very powerful tool that has been life transforming.

This book provides guidelines for successful treasure mapping based on twenty-plus years of my own and my clients' experiences with it. However, each reader will have a unique experience preparing for treasure mapping and applying the steps. The level of success you achieve will have a direct correlation to the extent of your belief in the process and in positive expectancy about your intentions. Are you interested in transforming your life? The choice is yours!

Summary

❋ You can make the choice to use treasure maps to represent what you want to have happen in your life.

❋ The Universe will repeat what you need to hear until you make the choice to pay attention.

❋ You need to make room for the goal you wish to accomplish.

❋ Treasure mapping is a powerful tool that you can use to transform your life.

Reflections

What choices have you made that became turning points in your life?

_____

_____

_____

_____

_____

_____

_____

_____

_____

_____

_____

_____

_____

_____

_____

_____

_____

Think of a time when you heard the same thing from different sources. What was the Universe trying to tell you?

_____

_____

_____

_____

_____

_____

_____

_____

_____

_____

_____

_____

_____

_____

_____

_____

_____

_____

_____

Chapter 2

Psychological Preparation: Reframing and Response-ability

All things are ready, if our minds be so.

William Shakespeare

If you've ever gardened, you've probably heard the saying "It's better to plant a $1 plant in a $5 hole than a $5 plant in a $1 hole." The point is: Soil preparation is everything. Once I lived in an area with clay-like soil—not very conducive to gardening. But I really wanted a garden, especially tomatoes, so I researched what to do to coax them to grow in such unfriendly circumstances. It turns out that if you prepare the ground by tilling sand, gypsum, and fertilizer into it, tomatoes will grow just fine, even in clay.

So it is when you begin treasure mapping. In order to create a fertile environment in which goal manifestation will occur, you need to be certain your thoughts are prepared. Philosophers through the ages have taught that our lives are reflections of our thoughts. In the words of Buddha, "We are what we think. All that we are arises with our thoughts. With our thoughts, we make our world." A similar statement that I first heard in the Unity church where my late-husband was a minister encapsulates the theory behind treasure mapping. It is called "the Law of Mind Action" and states: Thoughts held in mind produce after their kind.

Are you perfectly healthy? Do you find your career and personal life fulfilling? Are all your relationships harmonious? Is your life exactly the way you want it to be? Unless you are unusually fortunate, it is likely that there is some area of your life that you would like to improve. The simplest way to improve your life is to improve your thoughts. That is why, before you actually get started creating your treasure map, you will want to prepare your mind by "fertilizing" it with the idea that it is okay to ask for what you want. Have you ever said (or thought) statements like the following? [Fill in the blanks with something you have desired]:

I don't really deserve to have (or be)

_____

Who do I think I am to want

                                       ?
_____

It's selfish of me to wish for

_____

Thoughts like these can get in the way of successful goal achievement. For instance, if there is a part of you that says, "I would really like a career that makes a difference and gives me flexibility with my schedule" and another part of you that says, "Who do I think I am to want that?" or "I simply don't believe that it is possible," it will be very hard indeed for you to accomplish that goal.

For treasure mapping to be successful, especially if you notice yourself having these kinds of self-defeating thoughts, you will want to do some psychological preparation to get your thoughts in alignment with the concept of achieving your goals. This is a critical part of the treasure mapping process, and although it is simple, it is not necessarily easy. It may require a shift in the kind of thinking you have been doing all your life. In other words, you might have to do some reframing.

In a building where I once worked, there were several

large photographs hanging in the hallway. They were lovely pictures, but were simply mounted on poster board, hanging unframed. In an effort to spruce up the entrance to our office, someone decided to have the photos framed and re-hung. The transformation was remarkable! The entire hallway seemed brighter and more inviting. Perhaps you have had a similar experience of seeing the difference a frame can make in the appearance of a photograph or special work of art.

So it is when we reframe our thoughts about desiring or deserving prosperity, or anything else. Reframing can help people to see things differently, to feel differently about things or even to think differently. In his 1986 bestseller *Unlimited Power,* Anthony Robbins discusses the concept of reframing. Robbins says, "Reframing, in its simplest form is changing a negative statement into a positive one by changing the frame of reference used to perceive the experience." He recounts the story of a young boy who rode his bike, played baseball, and did everything young boys do—and was blind. His mother helped him reframe his blindness by telling him that he was seeing with his hands instead of his eyes, and reminded her son, ". . . there's nothing you can't do." So it is with us. Sometimes that which causes us pain, or appears to be a limitation of one kind or another, seems like an obstacle to our goal achievement. Yet, we can choose to see it as the source of our desire to change, and when we do, we achieve the results we want.

Let's go back to reframing prosperity. If the idea of desiring or deserving prosperity feels selfish to you, you can begin reframing that thought by asking yourself: "If I am lacking in any area of my life, am I always expressing my best possible self? Am I maximizing my full potential?"

To answer that, think about a time when you didn't have enough money to pay the bills, or when you had a relationship or job end unexpectedly, or when you simply did not feel one hundred percent healthy. Were you able to totally overcome any anxiety or sadness and be cheerful and loving to all you met? If you had financial concerns, did you call your creditors and confidently explain your situation? Did you maintain a patient and positive attitude with your co-workers and family? If you had health challenges, were you able to honor all your commitments to co-workers, friends, and family?

If you answer honestly, it is very likely that these stressful times created discomfort for you, which you in turn reflected in your interactions with others. You may have avoided answering the telephone or opening the mail, felt awkward and inferior around your friends, or felt guilty. Simply, you were not expressing your best self to your full potential.

Lack in any area of your life—health, relationships, career satisfaction, or any other area—prevents you from expressing your best, or highest, self. It creates stress, unhappiness, and possibly even more health challenges.

In fact, to accept lack in any area of your life is truly self-ish in the worst sense of the word!

Use this realization to help you reframe your thinking from "desiring prosperity is selfish" into "desiring and achieving prosperity enables me to express my highest self to my full potential!" From this perspective, desiring prosperity is healthy and important.

Reframing negative messages shifts our thinking from fear-based limited thinking, or lack-thought, to faith-based possibility—positive—thinking. As we learn to think and express ourselves in a more positive manner, we draw positive experiences to us. Further, we begin to take response-ability for our lives—literally, we have the ability to respond to life's challenges creatively.

One couple, faced with tremendous financial challenges, used reframing and response-ability in a practical way. They began keeping what they called their "Gratitude Journal." Every time they received any indication of prosperity, no matter how small it seemed, they wrote it in their journal. They reviewed their journal each evening, and as they did, gave thanks for what they did have instead of brooding with anxiety about their situation. Their thinking was shifting from fear-based to faith-based. Soon, new opportunities presented themselves, and before long, their financial condition was brighter.

Treasure mapping is grounded in a faith-based perspective. This doesn't mean you must subscribe to a particular religious denomination. On the contrary, it is about simply having faith that we live in a benevolent, abundant Universe, and that when we are intentional about our goals, we will accomplish them. We do not need to know how the goals will be accomplished, but we do need to have faith that it is possible.

> No matter how hard you work for success, if your thought is saturated with the fear of failure, it will kill your efforts, neutralize your endeavors, and make success impossible.
>
> Baudjuin

About the same time that I made my treasure map for a new partner, I made a list of other things that I wanted to do or accomplish. One of the items on that list was to take my children to Disney World. I had no clue how I would be able to afford this, but somehow I just knew it was possible. I had faith that it was. The very next year, Phil and I got married. Phil was a Unity minister, participating in committee meetings at the Unity convention, which that year was to be held in Orlando. We all went, and of course, took the children to Disney World! Yet, at the time I listed that as a goal, I could never have predicted how it would come to pass.

As you begin to work on shifting your thinking from fear-based to faith-based, notice your thoughts as you think about things you would like to do or have. If you find yourself thinking or saying things like, "That would be impossible" or "I could never do/have that," immediately stop that line of thinking (I knew one woman who would say aloud, "Cancel that thought!") and replace it with something like "This is an abundant Universe. This or something better is mine now." It sounds very simplistic, but it works. The challenge initially is to be ever vigilant about noticing unconstructive thoughts and substituting them with positive declarations.

> All personal breakthroughs begin with a change in beliefs.
>
> Anthony Robbins

Let's go back to the garden analogy. Once you have prepared the soil, it is equally important that you tend the garden—you need to water it regularly, fertilize it, and pull the weeds. Similarly, as you prepare your mind with the idea that it is okay to ask for what you want, you need to tend your thoughts—weeding those that are unproductive or negative. When I first made a treasure map for a new partner, it was all too easy to start thinking fearful thoughts—everything from "Why would anyone ever want to marry me?" to "What if I end up all alone in my old age?" This is where an affirmation was helpful. When I noticed myself having those fearful thoughts, I would repeat my affirmation a few times until the negativity subsided and I could let myself feel a little hopeful again. Later I learned about using denials with affirmations to help align my thinking even more. (There will be more about denials and affirmations in chapter 7.)

> Work in the invisible world at least as hard as you do in the visible.
>
> Rumi

People used to ask me how long I was single before I married Phil. When I answered, "Less than two years," they would practically scoff and say, "That's not very long." True, it wasn't long, but I was doing such intense mental "gardening" trying to shift my thinking from being fear-filled to faith-filled that it felt like a very long time. That's one reason why I say that treasure mapping is simple, but not easy. If you are a person who has had issues with asking for what you want, or who received "lack-thought" messages such as "there isn't enough," "it's too expensive," "we can't afford it," and/or messages about being selfish or undeserving, it will be essential for you to shift your thinking to a more faith-based perspective. This shift will maximize your treasure mapping experience; reframing can help you make that shift. Once you are comfortable with reframing, you will be ready to write a personal prosperity definition.

The indispensable first step to getting the things you
want out of life is this: decide what you want.

Ben Stein

The Importance of a Personal Prosperity Definition

By all outward appearances, David was a very successful
businessman. He managed his own thriving business and
lived with his wife and children in a beautiful suburban
home. What more could he want? David wasn't sure. He
only knew he was not happy with his life, and he wanted
something to change. David contacted me for a treasure
mapping consultation.

As he explained what was going on in his life, David
told me that he had taken over his father's business. In
his family, there was an unwritten work ethic that
required twelve-hour days and six-day weeks. Vacations
were out of the question. Dutifully, David worked these
long hours as his father had trained him. But his hard
work was beginning to take a toll on David's family life
and physical well-being. His wife and children com-
plained that they rarely saw him and that he was missing
family events. He suffered frequent headaches and had
been told by his doctor that he was a prime candidate
for an ulcer.

I asked David to define what prosperity meant to
him. His list included good health, family vacation time,

and time alone with his wife. Yet, his life did not reflect these desires. David was fulfilling his father's definition of prosperity. His father had started his business with little money when he was new to this country, and to him, prosperity simply meant being able to work hard and earn a lot of money. Now, even after the business was very successful and he could afford to hire others to help manage it, David was still pursuing his father's quest. Yet, both of David's parents had been dead for several years!

David's situation illustrates the importance of developing a personal prosperity definition. Just as successful businesses have mission statements as guides to help ensure that their practices are in alignment with their values and goals, we are able to create lifestyles consistent with our values and goals when we have defined what prosperity means to us on a personal level. Prosperity, as used here and throughout this book, encompasses all that fulfills you on every level of your life—spiritual, mental, emotional, and physical. It is a very individual and intimate thing. If you have been chronically ill, it is likely your definition will include perfect health. A person in recovery from substance abuse may top his or her list with "a serene and continuous sobriety." In addition, a personal prosperity definition is not static. In other words, it may change as your life circumstances change. For instance, when my children were young, my definition included having time to volunteer with their school activities. Now that they are adults, part of my definition includes: "maintaining close-knit, harmonious relationships with my children and their loved ones."

A final note on this topic—consider the last time you took a trip. One of the first things you did was decide where to go—a specific destination. If your plan was to fly from New York to Los Angeles, you didn't permanently disembark if your plane stopped in Chicago. Similarly, in your life journey, if you have a clear idea of what your prosperity destination is, you will set the wheels in motion to attain it—without settling for something that's just halfway there. So, if you define prosperity as making a good income, having good health and acquiring nurturing relationships, but, like David, are achieving only the good income, you are only part way to your destination. Writing a personal prosperity definition will help you get clarity about where you want to go with your life. Working through the steps of the treasure mapping process will help you get there.

> Failure to follow desire, to do what you want most, paves the way to mediocrity.
>
> Melody Beattie

Summary

❀ Treasure mapping is based on "the Law of Mind Action"—thoughts held in mind produce after their kind.

❀ Reframing negative messages and thought patterns can help you shift your thinking from fear-based to faith-based.

❀ As you act from a faith-based perspective, you are able to take response-ability for your life.

❀ Accepting lack in any area of your life prevents you from maximizing your potential and expressing your highest self.

❀ A personal prosperity definition enables you to create a lifestyle consistent with your definition.

Reflections

What messages have you received that might be preventing you from believing that you can achieve your goals?

_____

_____

_____

_____

_____

_____

_____

_____

How can you re-frame them with faith-based messages?

_____

_____

_____

_____

_____

_____

_____

_____

Exercise: Writing A Personal Prosperity Definition

Take a few moments to find a comfortable, quiet place
where you won't be interrupted. Now relax, and think
about what being prosperous means to you. How do
you feel as you experience prosperity? [Remember to
dismiss those thoughts about what prosperity would be
for your parents, your partner, your children, or how it
appears in the movies or a favorite novel.] After a few
moments, write your personal definition of prosperity.
Date the page. Revisit your definition every once in
awhile to make sure it still fits for you. Change it as
your life warrants.

Chapter 3

Treasure Mapping: An Adventurous Process

The great thing in this world is not so much where we are, but in what direction we are moving.

Oliver Wendell Holmes

When I conduct workshops on treasure mapping I frequently begin by asking participants to tell me what they know about treasure mapping and what their experiences have been with it. There is often a range of responses, from those who have no treasure mapping experience at all to those who report some measure of success with what they describe as "making a collage of what I want." To some extent, this description is accurate. A treasure map does represent a goal with pictures and words in a collage-type format. But more than that, treasure mapping is a unique goal-achievement process. Sometimes, when people hear "goal-achievement" they think of traditional goal-setting techniques and shudder; they find these techniques stifling and tedious. The good news is that in addition to eliminating the tedium, treasure mapping differs from traditional goal setting in a number of other ways.

Creating a treasure map is fun! It engages your playful spirit, that "dream-seeking child" within you who still believes in life's possibilities. Rather than specifying a series of tasks you will complete in order to accomplish your goal, you simply create an intentional "work of art" symbolizing your goal with an attitude of positive expectancy. You open your heart and mind to be guided about what to do and when to do it.

You do not need to determine how your goal will be accomplished. Once you have created your treasure map, you trust that you will be guided as to what you need to do to turn your goals into reality. In this sense, the treasure mapping experience enhances your ability to hear and respond to your intuition.

You do not need to determine when your goal will be accomplished. Remember, treasure mapping is based on the belief that thoughts held in mind produce after their kind. To help you hold your goal in mind, you will write an affirmation on your treasure map that your goal is achieved in the present tense. In other words, now! This prevents any self-imposed limitations from getting in the way and allows divine timing to occur. Repeating your affirmation that your goal is occurring in the present tense turns into an exercise in faith—trusting that when the time is right, the goal will be achieved. My experience in trusting divine timing is that typically goal achievement happens sooner than expected.

You do not need to determine the way in which your goal will be accomplished. You will specify the outcome you desire, but the manner in which your goal manifests may differ from your expectations. For example, one woman used a treasure map with a goal of creating a more nurturing work environment. She had a very good job and was not planning to quit, although it was a drain on her physically and emotionally. Within a week of creating her treasure map, she was laid off! This is not what she expected, but it was exactly what she needed to move on to a situation that was far more fulfilling for her.

Treasure mapping involves you on a number of different levels: emotionally, when you do the psychological preparation discussed in chapter 2; mentally, as you set your intention about what you wish to achieve and begin to trust your intuition; and spiritually, as you develop faith-based thinking and positive expectancy in divine timing and abundance of the Universe.

You may create a treasure map for absolutely

anything your heart desires, provided those desires are motivated by love and will not bring harm to another person or thing.

You can see that there are significant differences between traditional goal setting and this goal achievement process. There are also a couple of important ways in which treasure mapping is similar to traditional goal setting. Notice the word process. One meaning of "process" is "series of actions, changes, or functions that bring about an end or result." (*American Heritage Dictionary, New College edition*) Both methods require a process, or a series of actions, to obtain a result. And in both cases, application of the process is the responsibility of the individual. In traditional goal setting, one must determine timelines and complete specific tasks towards the accomplishment of the goal. In treasure mapping, once you are psychologically prepared to begin, there are five steps that you will sometimes "work" simultaneously. You will progress through these steps to facilitate manifestation of your goal. So, despite the significant differences in these two approaches to goal achievement, the bottom line is that both require a series of actions and are ultimately the responsibility of the individual to carry out.

Treasure mapping might also be described as a search or quest towards manifestation of a personal treasure. Thinking of it as a search or quest gives the process an air of adventure. Adventure is defined as "an unusual experience marked by excitement and suspense." That is a perfect description of treasure mapping: An adventurous process of goal achievement! It is an unusual method of accomplishing goals, and it can certainly be exciting and suspenseful. The very words "treasure map" conjure up images of crinkled drawings with X marking the spot where you might find gold coins, jewels, and perhaps even a few pirate bones. In a way, these images are accurate. In order to manifest your personal treasures, you may find that you must unearth a few skeletons. Skeletons such as fear, guilt, and resentment can be huge blocks to goal achievement, and they must be identified and released in order to get to the "treasure." This is not always easy to do, but it is exciting and can be suspenseful.

One person who demonstrated this ability beautifully was Bonnie. Bonnie was feeling stuck in a job that was not challenging and that she didn't enjoy. She was afraid to quit because she had recently gone through a divorce and had a lot of debt. As we talked, Bonnie expressed a tremendous amount of resentment towards her ex-husband, who had had an affair. She had been in counseling, which she quit because she didn't feel it was helping her in her efforts to work through the betrayal. Bonnie contacted me for a treasure mapping consultation to help identify the other blocks (besides the obvious resentment) that might be blocking her ability to move on with her life. We decided to meet at her home, where I discovered that she still had all the dining room furniture, china, crystal, and bedroom furniture that she and her husband had purchased while they were married. Being surrounded by all these things constantly reminded her of him, to the point where she wasn't even comfortable in her own house.

After I explained the treasure mapping philosophy to her, Bonnie made a choice. Although it was somewhat frightening, she sold or gave away almost everything she owned—all that she and her husband had purchased together. Shortly thereafter, Bonnie reported a remarkable increase in energy and a new outlook on life, including a willingness to continue counseling to work on forgiving her former husband. Within a few months, she found a different job at a higher salary, and that required travel—something she loved to do. She also furnished her apartment with lovely new furniture that suited her tastes. It wasn't many months later that Bonnie was in a new relationship as well. Had this been an exciting and adventurous process of goal achievement? Bonnie certainly thought so.

Clients usually have no problem with the description of treasure mapping as "a search or quest," but they are sometimes offended by the concept of it being a "manifestation of a personal treasure," mistakenly believing that personal treasure always means material or financial gain. But prosperity encompasses all that fulfills you on every level of your life. As mentioned earlier, your personal treasure truly is personal—an intimate desire that is meaningful to you. It may mean perfect health to one person, serenity to another, a romantic relationship to someone else. And because you and your life circumstances change, your idea of "personal treasure" will probably change as well.

Additionally, treasure mapping is a spiritual approach to personal and professional fulfillment. As you go through this process, you will undoubtedly gain new insights about yourself, realizing that in "working" the steps you enhance your ability to listen to your intuition. The root of the word intuition means to observe or watch. When you use your intuition, you are focused on observing your inner, or higher, spirit. You arrive at a knowing that you haven't figured out intellectually or analytically. Treasure mapping helps you develop your intuition, and as your ability to use your intuition develops and grows, so does your trust that Divine Order really is at work. Your faith is strengthened, because you realize your goals are manifesting in a way to support your highest good. Whatever way that turns out to be, you will realize that there is as much benefit in the process itself as there is achieving your goals.

Summary

Treasure mapping differs from traditional goal setting in a number of ways:

* It's fun—an adventurous process of goal achievement.

* It involves you emotionally, mentally, and spiritually.

* You don't determine how, when, or the way in which your goal will be accomplished.

* You can use it for anything your heart desires that is motivated by love and that will not bring harm to another person or thing.

* Treasure mapping is a process of steps, which you may "work" simultaneously.

* Treasure mapping results are the responsibility of the individual in terms of making the choice to set intentions, to have positive expectancy, and to release blame and other blocks such as guilt, fear, and resentment.

* Personal treasure refers to an intimate desire that is meaningful to you.

* Treasure mapping enhances your ability to listen to your intuition, to trust in Divine Order, and to strengthen your faith.

Reflections

What skeletons might you need to consider releasing in order to achieve your goal?

_____

_____

_____

_____

_____

_____

_____

_____

_____

_____

_____

_____

_____

_____

_____

_____

_____

_____

What is a personal treasure for which you would like to treasure map?

_____

_____

_____

_____

_____

_____

_____

_____

_____

_____

_____

_____

_____

_____

_____

_____

_____

_____

_____

_____

Chapter 4

Step One: Release

You must begin to form a vacuum,
in both inner and outer ways.

Catherine Ponder

Have you ever walked into an unfamiliar building or
space that simply "felt" good? Or had the opposite experience of going into a room or house that you couldn't
wait to escape because it made you feel uncomfortable?
You were experiencing the energy of your environment.
The Chinese practice of Feng Shui is the practice of creating harmonious environments. Feng Shui teaches us how
energy moves in our environment, and how we are
affected by that energy. In places where you felt good,
you probably sensed a positive flow of energy, while in
places where you felt uncomfortable energy flow was
probably somehow stifled or blocked. Students of Feng

Shui understand the importance of de-cluttering in order to keep the energy moving.

In a website article called "Feng Shui and the Spirit of Change," Stanley Bartlett writes:

> Feng Shui teaches us that less is more and getting rid of the old makes room for the new. Do not accept lack of money as an excuse for why you do not surround yourself in perfection and beauty. Money is simply a form of energy and exchange. Many who complain of a lack of money often are out of balance with the natural flow of giving and receiving and so they have no money but they have lots of possessions (holding on). When you free yourself of the holding on or attachments to your things then you often find that you start to receive in abundance from the Universe.

A friend of mine who is a Feng Shui practitioner and professional organizer uses a simple question to help her clients decide whether or not to keep an item. She asks, "Is it beautiful or practical?" If the item is neither, it is released. There is a distinct parallel with this concept and the first step of treasure mapping, which is: release from your life anything that no longer serves you.

It is logical that if our physical space is crowded, it

can be difficult to move around—just think of a congested freeway at rush hour. That same freeway at another time of day flows freely, and it takes much less time to reach your destination. It is the same within our homes and offices. When we have too many things, we may feel crowded or disorganized, and our movement towards our goals becomes congested. Eventually, we may get there, but it likely takes much longer than it would have had we created more space. Likewise, if we are "clogged" with unresolved thoughts or emotions— anger, jealousy, fear, blame, grief—it makes sense that our own energy flow is diminished.

Those people who are most successful manifesting the goals that they represent on their treasure maps are those truly willing to release their personal blocks. Blocks are any tangible or intangible barriers that literally stand in the way of your ability to achieve your goal—they are those things that are no longer serving you. Tangible blocks are physical "things" and can include almost anything you can think of from houses and real estate to furniture, clothing, jewelry, photographs, or as I mentioned in the first chapter—even old cards and letters. Intangible blocks are, typically, emotional attachments to the past, including any thoughts, memories, feelings, and/or attitudes that prevent you from being open to life's present and future possibilities. We'll look at some of these more closely later in this chapter. Inevitably, the tangible blocks are intertwined with an intangible emotion, so releasing the tangible facilitates the release of the intangible.

> I believe it's a fact of life that what we have is less important than what we make out of what we have.
>
> Fred Rogers

To determine whether or not a particular tangible item is a block for you, ask yourself your reason for keeping it. If your motivation is fear, guilt, jealousy, or similar emotion, that item is a block. Remember the story of Bonnie in the last chapter? She had a house full of things that she didn't really want but kept anyway because she didn't want her ex-husband to have them. Besides that, she felt bad with the stuff around, because it reminded her of her failed marriage. The furniture and other things symbolized her resentment towards her former spouse. It all became a tangible block, just as her resentment was an intangible block preventing her from moving on and receiving her good.

Simply, the motivation behind why you keep something is key to whether or not it is a block to your personal growth and prosperity. When the motivation behind keeping something is "pure" or unfettered by fear or negativity, it is not a block to prosperity. One client who contacted me wanted to create a treasure map for a new relationship. She was concerned because she had a number of photograph albums that included pictures of her former husband. When I asked her why she was keeping them, she replied that she wanted to be able to give them to her children and grandchildren when they were older. She was not keeping them out of anger or fear that she wouldn't ever be happy again. She simply wanted a history of her life to share with her family; releasing the albums was not necessary.

Intangibles

Intangible blocks can take many forms. There are the obvious ones like blame, resentment, anger, and jealousy —what we might describe as "negative" emotions— that often get in the way of establishing healthy relationships. But there are other traits and emotions that also block your ability to achieve your goals. These include perfectionism, worry, even memories or other kinds of emotional attachment to the past. Identifying and releasing one's personal blocks is key to goal accomplishment.

Once you recognize that you have an intangible block (or blocks), you are ready to begin the releasing process. It is probably not surprising that this often involves forgiveness—a major ingredient in block-release.

Forgiveness
There is a familiar story of a teacher who once told her students to bring a clear plastic bag and a sack of pota-

toes to school. For each person in their lives whom they felt had hurt them or towards whom they felt anger, they were to choose a potato. On it they wrote the person's name and date, and put it in the plastic bag. Some of their bags were quite heavy. They were then told to carry this bag with them everywhere for one week, putting it beside their beds at night, next to them on the school bus, under their desks at school. Naturally, the condition of the potatoes deteriorated to a nasty smelly slime. This, of course, made the students unpleasant to be around. They needed to be constantly mindful of the sacks—they didn't want to leave them in embarrassing places! It didn't take long for each of the students to figure out that the hassle of lugging the sack around was a metaphor for the price we pay for hanging on to anger and for being unforgiving. When we are unforgiving, or when we hold on to any negative emotion, we are unpleasant to be with and we carry with us a heavy weight. Carrying that weight depletes our energy. Getting rid of the weight is much more important than carrying it around. Forgiveness, and releasing negative thoughts and emotions frees us up. We are more energetic and are more pleasant to be with. Too often we think of forgiveness as a gift to the other person. Forgiveness, clearly, is for us. And forgiveness is one of the key tools in releasing intangible blocks.

It may be that throwing away a bag of rotting potatoes seems far easier than resolving some of the emotional issues in your life. Indeed, it may be much easier to release the tangible clutter than it is the intangibles, but my experiences and those of my clients indicate that even having the willingness to do the forgiving and letting go is a good start, and can begin to improve the energy flow.

Elisabeth Kübler-Ross, in addition to her work as physician and author, conducted workshops for people who were in crisis: terminally ill patients, parents of murdered children, Vietnam veterans, and others. She told a remarkable, true story about willingness to forgive. It is about a woman named Golda, whom she met after World War II at the concentration camp in Maidanek. Golda's father had been kidnapped by the Gestapo and was never seen again. She, her mother, brother, and sister had been sent to the gas chamber, but Golda survived when the chamber became too crowded and the guards couldn't squeeze her in. Kübler-Ross reported:

> I asked Golda what she was doing now. She said that when she was first liberated from the concentration camp, all she wanted was to get sweet revenge in some way. `But then it struck me that if I got revenge, I would be no better than Hitler himself,' she told me. And Golda said she was now working in a children's hospital in Germany. She said she had deliberately chosen to help German children—most of them war victims— to purge her bitterness toward the German

people. And she said she had come back to Maidanek, and she would stay at Maidanek until she had completely forgiven Hitler. `When I can do that,' she said, `then I'm allowed to leave.' . . . Golda taught me that it is our own personal choice whether we continue living as victims of hate and rage and the need for revenge or whether we see such tragedies as the windstorms of life and allow them to strengthen us and help us grow.

It is empowering to realize that forgiveness is a choice. When we choose to forgive, we claim our power, we become stronger, and we are able to move forward. To not forgive keeps us in a victim-consciousness, and as Golda stated we then are not much better than the perpetrator of the pain.

Sometimes, people will believe they have done a thorough job of releasing their blocks, creating their treasure maps and affirming that their goals are being achieved. But nothing appears to happen. This is a clue that forgiveness needs to take place.

The outward work can never be small if the inward one is great, and the outward work can never be great or good if the inward is small or of little worth.

Meister Eckhart

Emotional Attachment

Prosperity teacher Edwene Gaines discusses another way that the unwillingness to forgive keeps us in victim-consciousness. She maintains that where there is financial debt, there is unforgiveness—frequently of self— for real or imagined transgressions. We keep ourselves over-extended by buying what we want but subconsciously feel we don't deserve; being in debt is a way to punish ourselves and prevent total enjoyment of what we've acquired.

Staying in debt can also be one manifestation of an often subconscious desire to stay connected to our roots, particularly if those roots were in a fear-based or otherwise dysfunctional family system. In the early 1980s, a woman named Jael Greenleaf published a pamphlet called *Adult Children of Alcoholics*. She states, "For anybody who's grown up in a dysfunctional family . . . deprivation is the most emotionally familiar place there is. It doesn't feel good, but it does feel familiar, and anything that feels familiar is comforting . . . (it) reflects back a picture of yourself that you can recognize, a sense of knowing who you are. . . . And knowing who you are is primary for most people."

Even if alcoholism is not a factor in your family of origin, if your family system operated from a fear-based perspective, you are probably familiar with deprivation. That is, there is an atmosphere of "doing without," or, if you do get what you want, there is a sense of feeling guilty, especially if you go into debt to do so. Although you may not like the way it feels, it is familiar and you may subconsciously try to re-create that feeling as an adult. This becomes a subtle form of emotional attachment—an intangible block—that can prevent your success with goal achievement.

Surprisingly, even positive memories can block a successful treasure mapping experience. One of my clients was a widow who had been happily married for many years. She thought she felt ready to establish a new relationship, but as we talked, she frequently said, "No one will ever compare to my husband. He was wonderful!" This woman's memories of her husband were precious and very positive, and that's great. In order to open the way to a new relationship, however, it will be important for her to release the idea that no one could compare to her husband. As long as she is declaring that, she will be unable to see the possibilities for a relationship in anyone she happens to meet. Since she was unwilling to change her belief that no one would compare to her husband, it became clear that she wasn't as ready for a new relationship as she thought she was.

> You can't cross the sea merely by standing and staring at the water.
>
> Rabindranath Tagore

Perfectionism

Perfectionism is another intangible that blocks treasure-mapping success. You probably know the type—those individuals who set and try to maintain impossibly high standards for themselves (and often for their children, partners and/or employees) and who are displeased with anything less. Outwardly, they often seem to really have it "together" but my experience with people like this is they are seldom truly happy because things are just never "good enough" for them. Frequently, perfectionism stems from a conscious or unconscious need to prove one's worth to parents or other family members or to compare oneself with others and feel "better than" others. In any case, perfectionism can block successful goal achievement. One woman I worked with exhibited perfectionism in most areas of her life, but especially about her image. She exercised faithfully, spent thousands of dollars each year on salon services—to be buffed, waxed, massaged, coifed, manicured, and she always bought the latest fashions. Her home was also "perfect"—a veritable showcase for *House Beautiful.* Despite all this, (or perhaps because of all this?) she was one of the unhappiest people I ever met. Until people knew her fairly well, they would have a positive impression of her as someone who seemed to really have it "together." However, when we started to discuss her treasure mapping goal, she shared that she felt almost panicked about growing older, and she was disturbed by the fact that some of her family members tended to ignore her. Further, she had a pattern of making "best" friends who sooner or later disappeared from her life. She made the decision to try treasure mapping when an in-law finally told her that he didn't enjoy being around her because her focus was always about appearances— hers as well as other people's, and he often felt judged by her for not meeting her standards. His honesty, hard as it was to hear, helped her realize that her perfectionism and absorption with how she and her house looked actually prevented her from being a supportive friend and family member. She became willing to begin to release the notion that everything needed to be perfect, and she created a treasure map with a goal of being able to sustain harmonious relationships with friends and family. Clearly, a change like this is not going to happen overnight, but the recognition of the block and the willingness to release it are a significant start.

Worry

> Our doubts are traitors,
> And make us lose the good that we oft may win,
> By fearing to attempt.
>
> William Shakespeare

Another intangible block that prevents successful treasure mapping is worry. Remember the Law of Mind Action? Thoughts held in mind produce after their kind. That which we give attention to is what we create more of in our lives. The more you worry, the more you create to worry about. Have you ever had the experience of having something happen that you really didn't want to have happen, and then said to yourself, "I was afraid of that!" Thankfully, not everything we fear or worry about comes to pass, (just as everything we hope for does not), but worrying is counterproductive and, like other intangible blocks, needs to be released. A simple way to release worry is by using affirmations, which are discussed in more detail in chapter 7.

Worry was a major block for one woman who wanted to create a treasure map to buy a house. Before she even started working on the treasure map, she was expressing fear about how as a single woman she would qualify for financing, how she would manage to take care of the yard, what she would do if there were a major maintenance issue. On and on she went with concerns that *might* happen. She worked herself into such a frenzy worrying about all the "what ifs" that she chose not to make a treasure map. As a result, she stayed in an apartment she disliked—missing the chance to be in a home of her own and losing out on the financial rewards that home-ownership can provide.

Toxic People

In addition to releasing tangible and intangible items, you may need to let go of the toxic people in your life. Toxic people are those who drain you in some way— emotionally, spiritually, financially, or physically. They tend to be critical, judgmental, chronic complainers or simply negative thinkers—the "glass half empty" type of person who appears unwilling to take any action to change. They see limitations instead of possibilities, problems instead of opportunities, and difficulty instead of ease. People like this are unpleasant to be around, but almost all of us have had to associate with them at one time or another.

The reason we need to release them is that toxic people express negative energy. If this is directed towards you or something you are doing, it can be a barrier to your goal achievement.

When associating with toxic people, remember that "misery loves company" and that negativity can be contagious. Although it may be subconscious, toxic people will try to drag others down with them as validation for their complaints and inaction. When there is a person in your life who leaves you feeling drained and depressed rather than nurtured and supported, it is a clue their negativity is rubbing off, and it may be time to release them.

Use the Relationships Releasing Statement from exercise #1 at the end of this chapter to free yourself of toxic relationships. The release can be literal—as when you are releasing a negative co-worker and it turns out that you or that person changes jobs. Release can also occur in another way. Your perception of the person might change, or the person's negativity might no longer have any power to affect you. In any case, it won't be necessary for you to even let the other person know what you are doing—there will simply be a change in the relationship. You do not have to know how it will change, only be ready to accept that there will be change.

If the toxic person in your life happens to be your partner, spouse, or a family member, you may prefer to treasure map for harmony in your relationship rather than releasing the person from your life. You may also choose to treasure map for your own strength and confidence in dealing with that person, or as mentioned earlier, you might decide to treasure map for the ability to perceive the person differently or to release the power of the individual's negativity to have an impact on you.

Suppose you were bitten on the finger by a poisonous snake. You wouldn't angrily cut off your whole finger to be rid of the toxin. You would gently squeeze the wound to release the toxin. Likewise, as you release toxic people, do so gently, without anger or judgment.

To be wronged is nothing unless you continue to remember it.

A Course in Miracles

The adage "nature abhors a vacuum" is certainly true in the process of goal achievement. If your life is filled with tangible or intangible clutter, there is simply not room for your goals to occur. Once you remove the literal and emotional clutter, you will have created a vacuum "in both inner and outer ways" paving the way for goal manifestation.

Summary

❊ The first step in treasure mapping is to release whatever is no longer serving you. This is your opportunity to create the physical, emotional, and spiritual room for your good to flow to you.

❊ Blocks take many forms. They may be tangible things such as clothes, furniture, cards, books or they may be intangible, including negative emotions such as blame, fear, guilt, worry. Toxic people can also be blocks to goal achievement.

❊ Your motivation for keeping something tells you whether or not it is a block to your personal growth and prosperity.

❊ Forgiveness is key to releasing negative thoughts and emotions.

Reflections

List the tangibles and intangibles in your life that could
be blocks to your goal achievement.

Releasing Exercises

1. Releasing Statements

The following activity may be used for the release of tangible as well as intangible blocks. For tangible items, simply say the releasing statement aloud as you let go of the item, filling in the blank with the name of the item. (Letting go may include giving it away, selling it, burning it, ripping it up, or simply discarding it.)

Releasing intangible blocks is more of an intangible activity, and may require more persistence. Every day for 30 days, spend at least five minutes mentally repeating the statement below to release memories, feelings (such as anger, guilt, fear, resentment, jealousy) and/or ideas (I can't, I'm too old, it's impossible, etc.) that are preventing you from achieving your goals. Fill in the blank with the name of the block. If there are multiple blocks to eliminate, you may substitute "All that is preventing the achievement of my highest good" for the naming of a specific block.

Tangible / Intangible Releasing Statement:
"_____, I joyfully release you. I completely free you and let you go. You no longer serve my needs. As I set you free, I am free."

The following statement may be used to release toxic people as well as memories of past relationships that may be blocking your ability to establish healthy, significant new relationships.

Relationship Releasing Statement:
"I lovingly set myself free from everything and everybody that are no longer part of my plan to have all that I desire in life. Everything and everybody that does not support and nurture me, now release me. Only relationships that contribute to my highest good are part of my life now."

Write your own releasing statements:

_____

_____

_____

_____

_____

_____

_____

_____

_____

_____

_____

_____

2. Visualization

Another activity to use to release intangible blocks is to sit quietly with your eyes closed. Breathe deeply, exhaling anxiety and inhaling tranquility. When you are relaxed, think of a symbol to represent your intangible block—perhaps a monster or a chain, something that you perceive as negative. Now, imagine how you would like to make it disappear. Perhaps you pour some magic water on it and it evaporates. Perhaps you put it in the basket of a hot air balloon and send it sailing away. Maybe you touch it with a magic wand and it turns into a butterfly and flits away. Visualize the scene in as much detail as possible. What is the temperature? Is the sun shining? Are there any smells or tastes? The more vividly you can visualize the experience, the more thoroughly your block will be released. Notice how you feel as the symbol of your block vanishes. When your block has disappeared and you feel ready, open your eyes. Repeat this exercise as needed. Eventually, if the block returns into your mind, you will be able to quickly see it vanishing in the manner you have visualized and be able to permanently eliminate it from your life.

3. Forgiveness of Others

Find a quiet place, where you will be alone and uninter-rupted. Close your eyes and call to mind those people you want to forgive. You may choose to concentrate on one person or as many as you can think of. Mentally place one person at a time on a small stool in front of you, so the person needs to look up to you.

a. Tell that person how you feel about him or her and about how his/her behavior has affected you.

b. Acknowledge any desire to hurt or punish the person. You may wish to watch the person suffer for a moment, but then it is necessary to give up the desire for revenge and replace it with compassion. (To "forgive" means to "give for," or "give up." You are giving up revenge and replacing it with compassion.)

c. Say: "You, too, are a child of the Universe. Your own pain created the pain you caused me. Now, forgive-ness sets us free. All is well between us. I wish you suc-cess and prosperity."

d. Now see the person and yourself standing together, the same height, and looking eye to eye. Mentally, shake hands or embrace, if that feels right. Send the person on his/her way.

4. Forgiveness of Self

Perhaps there is an incident in your life about which you feel guilt or regret. It is time to forgive yourself. This activity is similar to the previous exercise, except it is yourself that you talk to. Note: Repeat the forgiveness exercises as often as you need to until you notice that you can think about what happened without feeling anger, guilt, or regret.

Go to a quiet place where you will be alone and uninterrupted. Close your eyes, and imagine how you looked when you were the age at which you want to forgive yourself. Mentally place that "you" on a small stool in front of you.

a. Tell yourself how you feel about you in terms of why forgiveness needs to take place. Talk about how your behavior has affected you.

b. Acknowledge any desire to hurt or punish yourself. Explain to your other self that it is that desire which has been contributing to the ways you have been abusing yourself (by over-eating, over-spending, smoking, not exercising, etc.).

c. Tell yourself you will now be giving up self-abuse for self-love.

d. Say: "I have always been and will always be a child of the Universe. I am forgiven and governed by love. I love myself and all that I have been and will be, past, present, and future. All is well."

e. Mentally embrace yourself. Invite that "You" into your heart, to live with you as a "built-in" support system.

Chapter 5

Step Two: Appreciating Who, What, and Where You Are

To accomplish great things,
we must not only act, but also dream;
not only plan, but also believe.

Anatole France

After losing a leg to cancer, Terry Fox jogged across Canada on an artificial leg in an effort to give hope to others dealing with the challenges of cancer. As the first black student to enter Central High School in Little Rock, Arkansas, Sybil Jordan Stevenson endured racist cruelties to graduate at the top of her class, going on to become a top level executive of a major corporation.

Winston Hong Lieu escaped from Vietnam when he was a teenager, leaving family and friends behind, and arrived in the United States speaking only a few words of English. A few years later, he graduated from high school near the top ten percent of his class and went on to earn a Masters Degree.

The list goes on. There are countless examples of people everywhere who have overcome seemingly impossible odds to achieve remarkable success. What is the common denominator among these people who attain their chosen goals despite tremendous challenges?

First, they believe in their ability to accomplish their goals. In his book, *The Power of Positive Thinking*, Norman Vincent Peale quotes Dr. Karl Menninger, who said, "Attitudes are more important than facts." Peale then goes on to tell a story of a time when he was golfing with a friend and he hit his ball into long grass. Peale remarked, "I am certainly in the rough!" His friend reminded him, "The rough is only mental . . . it is rough because you think it is. In your mind, you have decided that here is an obstacle which will cause you difficulty. The power to overcome this obstacle is in your mind. . . ." This reminder enabled Peale to make a beautiful shot all the way to the green. This is another example of The Law of Mind Action: Thoughts held in mind produce after their kind. People who accomplish their goals don't believe in "the rough." They do believe in their own ability to overcome.

Another characteristic of successful people is the ability to appreciate who, what and where they are in the present moment. This became the second step in the treasure mapping process as I witnessed the differences between people who were having success with their treasure mapping goals and those who seemed to have more difficulty manifesting their desires. Repeatedly, the folks who were able to appreciate whatever circumstance life handed them, or at least have a willingness to learn the lesson in the situation, were those who were most successful achieving their goals. In workshops on treasure mapping, I tell participants that I call this the "Count Your Blessings" step. Appreciating your circumstances allows you to seize the opportunities presented by your unique challenges and to make the most of them. Attitudes are more important than facts.

A dramatic demonstration of this is the story of Aron Ralston. He was the young hiker whose arm became trapped between a boulder and a canyon wall. After six days of entrapment, Aron performed the unthinkable—he amputated his own arm with a dull pocketknife, rappelled down a seven-story cliff and hiked for miles until he met a family who led him to his rescuers. His attitude helped him survive—despite the fact that for six days his arm was pinned, he ran out of food and water, and he had told no one where he was going. Just six months after the accident, he told Tom Brokaw in an interview that this was a profound spiritual experience, changing him at such depth that he would endure it again.

While this is a marvelous example of someone who made the best of a seemingly impossible challenge, it is also a wonderful metaphor for the miraculous outcomes that can occur when we free ourselves from the "boulders" in our own lives.

What kinds of boulders get in the way of your ability to appreciate your life in the present moment? First, you may be taking your life for granted. Second, you could be wishing it—or some aspects of it—were different in some way. In either case, these undesirable attitudes are your personal boulders because they directly conflict with your ability to achieve your goals.

People who take life for granted tend to get so caught up in the day-to-day "busy-ness" of life that they forget to notice the miracles occurring all around them—the sun coming up each day, a child's laughter, even the wonder of technology that allows us to almost instantly communicate with people all over the planet.

Sometimes, I will work with people who are actually a little stumped when I ask them what they can appreciate about their lives. And perhaps they really do have many challenges in their lives, but I will ask, "Can you breathe? See? Hear? Talk? Smell? Feel?" It may be that it comes down to the very basics for which we are grateful, and then we can build from there.

The second thing you might be doing if you are not appreciating who, what, and where you are in the present moment is wishing some part of you or your life were different. This generally takes the form of complaining. Even if you don't say it to other people, your thinking follows these lines:

"If only I weren't so _____ (fat, skinny, old, young, short, tall, poor)."

"I'll be happy when I _____ (can quit this job, lose some weight, have a baby, the kids move out, find the right partner, move to a different state)."

As long as you are focused on what you perceive to be negative about your life, it will be difficult for you to manifest what it is you want. Remember: Thoughts held in mind produce after their kind. In order for anything to become manifest, someone has to think about it first. Everything, from the chair you are sitting in to the space shuttle, was an idea—a thought in someone's mind— before it came into being.

It is the same for your goals. As you think about what is positive in your life, you set in motion your ability to create more of that into your life. Conversely, if you are concentrating on what is **not** working, you may inadvertently be attracting more of that into your life. Having said that, it is important that you pay attention to the messages your situation is providing.

Let's say your definition of prosperity includes good

health, a satisfying job, and a nurturing relationship. If you don't appear to be physically well, first ask yourself what is there about your body that you *can* appreciate, and be grateful for those things. Then ask your body what message it has for you. Do you need more sleep? Do you need to eat a healthier diet? Do you need more exercise? A chiropractor friend once told me that physical symptoms are a gift from the body to help us address the issue and heal sooner. It makes sense—think of a time you took extra vitamin C to help ward off a cold, and did in fact lessen the severity of the cold.

If you are struggling with a chronic or degenerative disease, and the reality is that your body probably won't get better, you may find it hard to appreciate anything about your physical situation. I invite you to consider the words of a wheelchair bound woman I know, who says, "I can still see, so I can read and keep current on the news of the world by watching television. I can hear, and I can speak to the people I care about. One of my arms and neither of my legs work, but my mind does, and for that I am grateful."

If you are wishing you were in a different job, think about the aspects of your present job that you can appreciate. Are you learning a skill that will be helpful in other jobs? Are you meeting people who will become long-time friends? Is your paycheck helpful in meeting expenses? If you are seeking a nurturing relationship, start by deciding what you appreciate about yourself. In fact, over the years it has become abundantly clear to me that loving yourself is a key factor in attracting love to you. You can also identify characteristics you would like in a partner by being aware of behaviors in past relationships you would like to have more of, or that you would not accept. You can appreciate even unsatisfactory conditions for helping you discern specifically what you do want!

By the same token, when you are focused on what isn't "working" in your life, or wish for what you don't have, you are giving energy to the negative or to the lack-thought. Have you heard the expression "When it rains, it pours?" When things aren't going well, they sometimes get worse before getting better. This is because the more energy you give to fear, worry, anxiety, the more power you give it. When something negative happens, an expectancy of more of the same creates just that. Not only do you increase your chances of creating more of the negative, you deprive yourself of the ability to use that energy more productively—for appreciating all that you are and all that is right in your world.

It is important to note that I am not suggesting you deny or suppress any strong feelings such as grief or justified anger in order to pretend you appreciate the way things are for you. In fact, it is essential that you process these kinds of emotions as a prerequisite to being capable of appreciating your life in the present moment. You may find you need help with this, and you may want to go to a licensed therapist or join an appropriate support group to sustain you in this effort. Appropriately dealing with and healing deep-seated emotional wounds is a healthy way to purge "negative clutter" to create room for your good to come in. It reminds me of a time when I smashed my finger in the car door. My broken finger was incredibly painful, and I felt more than a little frightened when the doctor said he would have to lance it to release the blood building up under the nail. But it was essential that blood be expressed to relieve the pressure and some of the pain so the healing process could begin. Later, the nurse told me that the nail on that finger would grow in stronger than it had ever been—and she was right. Likewise, when we have painful life experiences, we may need to seek professional assistance to help us express our emotions so we can begin to heal and become stronger too.

The people mentioned at the beginning of this chapter are vivid examples of individuals who understood the importance of appreciating their circumstances. Any one of them could have chosen to move into "Pity City," feeling sorry for themselves and focusing on the cancer, the injustice, or the loneliness. Instead, they used what they had and made the best of it, and in so doing, triumphed. You can, too!

Once you have an awareness that your own attitudes

may be blocking your path to success, there are three techniques you can use to change your attitude and start appreciating who, what, and where you are right now:

1. Use self-talk to your advantage
2. See your situation differently
3. Live in the present

Use Self-Talk to Your Advantage

Self-talk simply is what you say when you talk to yourself. Self-talk always reflects your attitude and beliefs. Since you spend more time each day talking to yourself than anybody else, it is logical that what you are saying to yourself will have an impact on your emotions and even on how you feel physically. In fact, in a July 1993 article in the *ERIC Clearinghouse on Reading, English, and Communication Digest* #84, Julia Wielke writes:

Communication and medical professionals have researched the psychophysiological components of self-talk, to conclude that what people say to themselves [affects] their ability to combat and ward off illnesses. Individuals can tap into the power of their own self-talk by recognizing it for what it is, reducing harmful negativity, and increasing the number of positive internal messages. . . . Thought patterns generated by self-talk affect health-states. What studies have shown has been supported by doctors and patients alike. People can begin to harness the power in their minds by taking an active role in deciding what to think, enhancing the positive messages they send themselves. It also involves being realistic; identifying the causes for any negativity, realizing it is a signal to act. By doing so, people can face challenges—health related or otherwise—with the knowledge they can succeed if they literally "put their minds to it."

Perhaps you believe that heart disease runs in your family. You could have the attitude that there's nothing you can do to prevent heart disease, so you might say to yourself, "I can't do anything about it. I'm going to die at an early age no matter what I do." Consequently, you choose to eat whatever you want, you don't bother to exercise, and you are not surprised when you experience a heart attack at a young age.

On the other hand, you might use the knowledge that heart disease runs in your family as a signal to act. In this case, you believe that heart disease can be prevented and your self-talk is, "I am staying healthy. I make wise choices and take care of myself." Based on what you tell yourself, you eat appropriately, exercise, and remain healthy. You are using self-talk to your advantage.

Self-talk is a valuable tool to use in the process of goal achievement. Used in a positive manner, it will keep you focused and calm. There is a self-talk exercise at the end of this chapter to heighten your awareness about what you have been saying to yourself, the feelings you had, and what resulted from what you said.

> Two men looked out of prison bars.
> One saw mud, the other saw stars.
>
> Anonymous

See It Differently

Phil enjoyed using *Chicken Soup for the Soul* stories to make a point in his sermons. One of his favorites was about two little boys named Grins and Grumbles. One version goes like this: Two brothers named Grins and Grumbles went to visit their Grandpa on his farm. As soon as they got there, Grumbles started to complain that there was nothing to do. So Grandpa told the boys that if they cleaned out the horse stable, they would get to ride the pony. That sounded great! So Grins and Grumbles dashed off to the stable where they found an enormous pile of horse manure and two shovels. The two boys picked up the shovels and got to work. Within minutes, Grumbles began to moan about how smelly it was, how hot he was getting, and what hard work shoveling was. Grins didn't pay any attention to him; he kept shoveling away, all the while doing a little dance and singing to himself. Grumbles couldn't believe that even someone as dorky as his brother could think shoveling manure was fun. "What are you so happy about?" he asked Grins. "With this much crap, we'll be here all day!" Grins smiled and replied, "With this much crap, there's got to be a pony in here somewhere!"

Our perceptions about life have as much to do with how we see as what we see. How do see your stable? If your life seems overflowing with challenges and difficulty, can you find a way to look at it differently, to see the pony instead of the manure? Although there is no magic formula for helping you understand why your life is the way it is right now, it is helpful to remember that there is a lesson in all that occurs. Whatever your circumstances, they are a gift to you. If you are willing to learn from your experiences, you will understand them at some level. When you refuse to learn, you will not understand—and the lesson will be repeated in one way or another. That's why so many of us find patterns in our lives—we grow up in an alcoholic home and marry an alcoholic; we continuously choose unavailable people as love interests; we repeatedly find jobs with demeaning, abusive bosses or co-workers. Until we break the cycle by learning what we need to from the experience, the pattern will continue in one form or another. One way we can learn to break the cycle is by listening to what the circumstances of our lives are saying.

Silent = Listen

The words "silent" and "listen" use exactly the same letters. This strikes me as an excellent reminder that when there is something going on in my life that I don't particularly like, it is time for me to get silent and listen. You can do this anywhere, anytime. The key is to be able to turn off the mental chatter, so that you are listening not to the day's "to do" list or the other thoughts racing around in your head, but to simply ask the question, "What is the lesson in this?" and listen with an open mind and heart. Perhaps you can do this as you take a walk, shower, or drive to work. If meditation is a part of your routine, maybe you will prefer to listen during that time. At the end of this chapter is an exercise to help you get silent and listen. As simple as this part of the treasure mapping process would seem, it is not always easy.

Phil used this technique after a series of mishaps. Within six months after buying a new car, he was involved in two minor accidents. In addition, the stereo he had installed in the car after the second accident was stolen from the car two weeks later. Frustrated at not understanding why these things were happening, he spent some time in silence to discover what it was he was to learn.

As he meditated, listening, his mind went to his work. Thinking this was some of that mental chatter, he re-focused on his breathing. Again, he heard work-related messages. Going with the flow of his thoughts, it occurred to him that he had been allowing people to invade his personal space at work. He had been accepting office telephone calls and appointments at home and was spending more and more time at the office in order to accommodate other peoples' schedules, missing his own personal commitments to do so. At first glance, this seemed unrelated to the incidents involving the car. What he came to realize, however, was that he was not doing a very good job of setting boundaries about work-related issues. Since he hadn't been aware of this on a conscious level, the "lesson" was being made clear with his car. In fact, the car represented how his personal space was literally being invaded. With this understanding, he began to set specific boundaries. He had no further car issues for a long time after that.

> Learning to live in the present moment is part of the path of joy.
>
> Sarah Ban Breathnach

Live In The Present

There is an old adage that tells us, "You can't change the past, but you can ruin the present by worrying about the future." This is important to remember as we seek to appreciate our circumstances. When we are consumed with regret about the past or anxiety about the future, we are blind to that which is positive about the present.

One of my clients felt she had made a poor choice, years earlier, regarding her career. She so deeply regretted it that, despite the fact she had held a series of positions with progressive responsibility, she couldn't appreciate the excellent experience and transferable skills she'd acquired. As we investigated what it would take for her to transition into the career she really wanted, she was surprised and delighted to learn that much of what she had done would be applicable in her new field. With a little specialized training, she would be ready to move into her new career.

Just as regretting the past is an exercise in futility, so too is worrying about the future. Besides being non-productive, worry can contribute to sleeplessness and its associated health problems. One way to help eliminate worry about the future is to concentrate on living—and being the best we can be—in the present moment. In the words of Emmett Fox, one of the most influential New Thought authors of the twentieth century, "The art of life is to live in the present moment, and to make that moment as perfect as we can by the realization that we are the instruments and expression of God Himself."

You can use the Releasing Exercises at the end of chapter 4 to help you eliminate worry and anxiety about the future and regrets about the past. Using the Releasing Exercises in conjunction with affirmations like those suggested at the end of this chapter will enhance your ability to appreciate who, what, and where you are on your path. Remember the garden analogy in the second chapter? Think of this step as tilling and fertilizing the soil. As you become more and more aware of your lessons and appreciative about your life, you are preparing to plant the seeds of your desires so you can manifest your dreams.

Summary

❈ Successful people believe in their ability to attain their goals.

❈ Those who experience the most success with treasure mapping are able to appreciate who, what, and where they are in the present moment.

❈ Appreciating your circumstances allows you to seize the opportunity presented by your unique challenges and make the most of them.

❈ Attitudes are more important than facts.

❈ Taking your life for granted or wishing it were different are attitudes that directly conflict with your ability to achieve your goals.

❈ Three techniques that will help you appreciate your circumstances are:
　　1. use self-talk to your advantage
　　2. see it differently
　　3. live in the present

❈ Grief and similar, intense emotions must be acknowledged and processed before one can truly appreciate his or her circumstances.

❈ Get silent and listen to learn the lessons of your situation.

Reflections

What situation in your life would you like to see differently? What is the lesson in the situation?

_____

_____

_____

_____

_____

_____

_____

_____

_____

_____

_____

_____

_____

_____

_____

_____

_____

Exercise: Get Silent and Listen

Set aside a few minutes in which you can just sit in total silence. Invite whatever it is that you need to become aware of to become clear to you, so that you can understand your lesson. Don't worry if you can't seem to stop thinking about things you feel are unrelated to your lesson. Let them come, and continue to concentrate on being still. You will find that as you seek silence on a habitual basis that the "busy" thoughts diminish in frequency or that they are, in fact, related to what you need to know. You may find that journaling your thoughts provides you with additional insight. Jot down notes on what you hear:

_____

_____

_____

_____

_____

_____

_____

_____

_____

_____

Exercise: Self-Talk

This exercise will heighten your awareness about what you have been saying to yourself and about any attitudes you may have that could be preventing you ability to successfully attain your goals.

Make a form similar to the following example. Over the next five days, keep track of what you say to yourself in various situations. After five days, reflect on how each situation might have been different (either more positive or negative) if your self-talk had been different (either more positive or negative). Are there any changes you would like to make in the way you talk to yourself? What are they?

Situation

_____

What I said to myself

_____

_____

How I felt

_____

_____

Result

_____

_____

Exercise: Affirmations

Say the following affirmations either aloud or to yourself to help you begin to appreciate who, what, and where you are in the present moment. Remember, to affirm means "to make firm." Saying affirmations establishes what you are saying as a definite part of your reality.

"I believe I can achieve my goals."

"I am willing to learn the lesson in this situation."

"My life is getting better and better, every day in every way."

"I am grateful that I can _____"
(Idea starters: wake up in the morning; take a shower; walk; talk; breathe; read; see my child's smile . . . the list is infinite, isn't it?)

Chapter 6

Step Three: Creating Your Treasure Map

If one advances confidently in the direction of his dreams, and endeavors to live the life which he has imagined, he will meet with success unexpected. . . .

Thoreau

This is the step for which you have been preparing, and other than seeing your goals become reality, it is certainly the most enjoyable. So far we have been concentrating on the inner work that is an integral part of the treasure mapping process: coming to terms with your own definition of prosperity and recognizing that you truly deserve it; releasing any blocks that might prevent you from attaining prosperity; and appreciating your present circumstances. All of these aspects of the process call for significant introspection and perhaps some rather emotional shifts in your thinking. Now, however, it is time to reawaken the dream seeker inside of you and have a little fun. In fact, imagine that you are inviting your inner child out to play!

First, a description of what a finished treasure map looks like might be helpful. It can actually take a variety of forms. The most common is a collage-like treasure map, consisting of pictures and words cut from magazines and glued on construction paper or poster board. See the next page for an example.

The sample treasure map represents a goal for greater physical fitness. The picture of the woman looks happy and active; the healthy meal depicts the way in which she would like to eat; and the butterfly represents transformation and Spirit. The words she has chosen describe the way she intends to feel as she accomplishes her goal. Her affirmation, *Today and every day, I am healthy, energetic, slender and strong* is short enough that she can easily repeat it frequently, yet is all encompassing enough for this particular goal.

Other ways to create your treasure map include:

A treasure map mobile—hanging fabric or paper symbols from a branch or other three-dimensional object;

A treasure map wreath out of grapevines or other material and tying or gluing symbols of your goals to the wreath.

Sample Treasure Map

A treasure map is always representative of your own creativity and is a very personal expression of who you are, so it is important you are comfortable with the media you use. Naturally, the more complex your treasure map is, the more time-consuming it will be to make— something to remember if you tend to procrastinate. If you are a procrastinator, it might be wise to start with a simple collage-type creation in order to set the process in motion. My very first treasure map, for a new partner, was one picture glued onto pink construction paper. Once I found the picture—a couple standing together looking very much in love—the map probably took me less than fifteen minutes to make, including writing my affirmation. So you see, the treasure map can be a very basic creation, and the only limit as to how it will look is your own imagination.

If the idea of a collage or mobile serving as the vehicle for goal achievement seems simplistic, ask yourself: Is my life precisely the way I want it right now? If it isn't, now ask yourself: What is the worst that can happen if I do create a treasure map? Maybe you'll spend a few dollars on a magazine or two, some poster board and a glue stick—but nothing in your life seems to change. It's more likely, however, that you will gain some clarity about what your goals are and you will have fun creating a visual representation of them. Even better, there will be some kind of energy shift that occurs and your life will begin to align more closely with your goals.

Remember that much of this process has to do with positive intentionality. In other words, consciously choosing your goals, being intentional about how you represent them, and having a sense of positive expectancy about achieving them are significant parts of the process. Also, treasure maps work on the subconscious level. Every time you look at your map, your goals and affirmations will be imprinted on your subconscious mind. In turn, your subconscious will steer you along the path towards goal achievement—perhaps you will get a "notion" to do something and discover that by doing it, you are progressing toward accomplishing your goal. It will appear that things are occurring in serendipitous fashion, but it is actually the shift in energy you have created in your world through treasure mapping.

There is no one "right" method in creating a treasure map. Keep in mind that a treasure map is your specific request to the Universe for what you want to have in your life. Therefore, each treasure map will be as unique as each request. There are, however, a few general guidelines that seem to facilitate manifestation:

Include a picture or symbol of your spiritual source. Whatever you perceive the source of your spiritual nourishment to be, include a representation of it on your treasure map. This is important because it reminds you that you do not need to determine "how" your goals will become reality for you. You are being clear about what it is you desire, and you are also clear that your trust is in the Universe to support you in attaining what you desire. The source symbol is a graphic way to "Let Go and Let God." You are demonstrating that you are doing your part and are now ready to give up controlling the situation. You will begin accepting help from the Universe.

Include a picture of yourself on the treasure map. You can use a photograph or draw a picture of yourself, but the idea is to visually connect yourself with the goal. Remember, your treasure map programs your subconscious mind, so each time you see your own picture with your goal achieved, it reinforces the belief that you can achieve this goal.

Focus on one goal per treasure map. Often when I teach treasure-mapping workshops, people want to know how many goals they can put on a map. What I have found over the years is that initially, it seems to be more effective to start with just one goal per map, and just one map. When you are focused on one particular goal, you can more readily recognize the lesson that will come up or healing that needs to take place, attend to it, and move on. Focusing on one goal will also help you to prioritize your goals and to get a "feel" for what it would be like to achieve your goal. After a few successes and a sense of how the process works for you, you may choose to create more than one map, still focusing on one goal per map. In fact, some people create several collage-type maps and put them in a large spiral-bound notebook.

They simply turn to the page on which they wish to concentrate on any given day.

Use a contingency clause. A familiar maxim says, "Be careful what you pray for, you might get it!" Similarly, some people are reluctant to create treasure maps because they believe that by being specific about what they want, they may be limiting their good. That is why I advise using a contingency clause, such as "This, or something better, is mine now." This eliminates any limits you might unknowingly be creating by being "too" specific.

Use color. There are different schools of thought on what specific colors symbolize. Two of these approaches are described here, but since you are the one who will be looking at your treasure map most often, it's important to use color that is aesthetically appealing to you.

In *The Dynamic Laws of Prosperity,* Catherine Ponder refers to the ancient science of color, suggesting that specific background colors (the poster board, paper, etc.) are most productive for specific results. They are as follows:

Green for career or financial prosperity
Blue for intellectual accomplishments (such as
    writing a book or going to school)
White for increased spiritual understanding
Bright yellow or *orange* for health and increased
    energy and vitality

> *Pink, rose,* or *warm red* for romance and/or har-
> mony in human relationships

When we conduct workshops that teach the paral-
lels of treasure mapping and feng shui, we discuss the
colors of the "bagua," which is usually an eight-sided
figure with a ninth area at center, superimposed over a
floor plan. In the workshops, we lay out the treasure
maps as though they were a bagua. The purpose of the
bagua is to define the nine areas of human life that are
affected by energy flow within the floor plan. The nine
life situations are defined as wealth, fame, relationships,
creativity, children, helpful people, career, knowledge-
spirituality, family, and health. Again, the suggestion is
to focus on the one aspect of your life that you would
most like to transform, representing how the other
areas of your life will be affected when you achieve
your goal. The following colors are used to represent
these nine different aspects of your life:

> *Green*—family of origin; community
> *Blue*—intellectual accomplishments; self-improve-
> ment; knowledge
> *White*—family you create; creativity; increased
> spiritual understanding
> *Yellow* or *Orange*—health and increased vitality
> *Pink, Rose*—harmony in relationships; romance;
> partnerships

Red—fame; reputation; how you are perceived by
the world

Violet, Purple—abundance; wealth; knowing the
Universe will provide

Black—career success; passions; anything about
which you want to be passionate

Gray—helpful people; travel; attracting people
who would be helpful

However, I know of people who felt other colors
were more inspirational and created treasure maps using
a wide variety of different colors. Once again, this is a
very personal project. You need to go with whatever
speaks to your heart.

It's also important to note that the colors you use to
represent your goals can be significant. For instance, I
had one client who found a newspaper picture of a car
she wanted printed in black and white. She put the
newspaper photo on her treasure map, and a few weeks
later someone offered her that model car at a very good
price. The only trouble was—the car was gray (like the
newspaper photo) and she wanted red! Someone else,
working on a significant relationship, cut out a picture
of a man with sandy brown hair, graying at the temples.
Within a few months, she was dating a man whose hair
was exactly that color.

*Include an affirmation that the goal you have
"mapped" for is yours—in the present tense.* This

establishes, consciously and sub-consciously, that what you want, you have. You are "holding this thought in mind and it will produce after its kind." This is a definite message to the Universe that you are willing to walk through any doors that open that might lead you to your goal. You are ready to take the responsibility to change.

Note, too, that because you are writing in the present tense, there is no need to include a date by which your goal will occur. You might prefer to declare something like, "This goal is mine through the right channels, at the right time." Do put the date you create your map on the back though, just to see how quickly your goals are achieved. See chapter 7 for more about affirmations in general.

Include a "thank you" to your spiritual source. A thank you is your affirmation of trust that your goal is being accomplished. It is as if you are declaring to the Universe or your higher power that you know you are working in partnership. You set the intention, create the map, and are willing to act on the messages you receive. The Universe provides the pathways by which you will reach your destination. A thank you to your spiritual source acknowledges the true source of your supply and fulfillment. Further, being conscientious about being grateful helps you prepare to receive, a sometimes surprisingly challenging thing to do. Finally, when you give thanks, you demonstrate appreciation for all that you receive, so you don't take life's blessings for granted.

Keep it private. When you write in a journal or diary, you probably keep what you write to yourself. Likewise, your treasure map represents an intimate part of who you are and you may choose to keep it private. If you do show it to others, it is best shared only with those who believe in the power of this process, and who will nurture and support you in your efforts to achieve your goals through treasure mapping. Negative comments from friends can be real blocks to our ability to believe that we deserve and can have whatever we put on our map, so it is unwise to show your map to anyone who will be less than positive. By the same token, put your map where you can see it often; hang it in a private place where you will see it regularly—the back of your bedroom door, inside your closet door, on the mirror of your private bathroom.

One of my male clients, who was a construction worker, opted to keep his map on a clipboard in his truck, since he drove alone a long distance each day to get back and forth from his construction site. By the way, he reported a significant shift in energy within a few weeks of affirming his treasure map while he was driving. Previously, he had been consumed with worry about the things in his life that weren't going well, which left him feeling somewhat depressed and fatigued.

The energy shift he experienced enabled him to pursue the leisure-time activity that was his goal.

Representing Intangible Goals

When your goal is a new car, it is relatively easy to find the picture of the car you want and paste it on your treasure map. But what if your goal is something like better health, happiness, or inner peace? You can't exactly open a magazine and find a picture of happiness. However, you can look for pictures that represent happiness to you—perhaps a puppy, a balloon, wild flowers. Again, this is a very personal experience, and you need to use symbols that fit your definition of your goal.

One woman was treasure mapping for a job change because she wanted to be in what she described as a "lighter" environment. At the office where she worked, she sensed heaviness—negative co-workers and an oppressive manager—and she wanted to have a more nurturing, positive work atmosphere. She found a picture of a floating feather, which she glued onto a picture of a desk to represent "lightness."

Keep in mind that part of the purpose of this process is to help you identify how you will feel once you have achieved your goal, so use pictures and words that represent different sensory experiences for you. If your goal is to feel more balance in your life, choose a color that you might associate with balance. Or choose a smell. A taste. A physical impression. Find pictures that symbolize those sensations and use those on your map. The more you can feel what it will be like to achieve your goal, the easier it will be to say your affirmation with conviction and the more powerful your treasure map will be.

This brings up an important point: Your conscious mind must believe to some degree that the goal on your treasure map is attainable. It is perfectly acceptable that your goal be something of a stretch from your present frame of reference, but you must also perceive it as realistic.

Healing Your Issues

As mentioned earlier, treasure mapping is not a sequential procedure in which you complete one step and move on to the next. Even after you have created your treasure map you will continue to become aware of blocks that need to be released. In fact, it may seem that—once your map is created—every possible barrier to your success surfaces. The Universe is not testing you. It is actually the shift in energy you create when you focus on your goals. The barriers that arise are your issues that need healing. In all likelihood, they will correspond directly to the goal represented on your treasure map.

One man experienced this phenomenon after creating a treasure map for more balance in his life. Within one week of making his treasure map, he was laid off of a job he had had for more than five years. To make matters worse, he was turned down for the first few jobs to which he applied. Initially, he was devastated. We discussed what the related issue might be that needed healing to help him move forward. He recognized that all of his self-esteem came from who he was at work; his identity came from having a powerful position in a highly regarded organization. He realized that part of his need to appear so successful in his work had to do with the fact that he was trying to prove his worth to other people; he wasn't very happy with the rest of his life—in particular the fact that he didn't have a significant relationship. Perhaps the blocks he was running into (the employment rejections) were a nudge from the Universe to develop some interests and relationships outside of work, which, in turn, would develop the balance for which he had treasure mapped. Shortly after he accepted this idea and became open to the possibility of taking a "less important" job, he became eligible to attend a training he had long wanted but had never had the time to do. Interestingly, he met a woman at the training whom he began to date. His goal of achieving more balance was manifesting in ways he could not have predicted.

Whatever personal issue surrounds the accomplishment of the goal most likely will appear as an obstacle. When you are open to this, recognize it, and deal with it, you pave the way to successful goal achievement.

The adventure of treasure mapping gives you the opportunity to address issues you may have chosen to suppress in the past. If this idea frightens you, I invite you to go back in time for a moment. Remember when you were a small child playing Hide-and-Seek? Whether you were hiding, waiting to be found, or seeking, hoping to find, there was that thrilling sense of anticipation preceding discovery. Your heart raced, maybe your palms got a little sweaty, and there were always delighted screams when the "seeker" made the find. Now, relate the treasure mapping experience to playing a game of Hide-and-Seek by yourself. You are seeking to accomplish new goals, but there are some things you need to discover first. Let your inner child guide you with a sense of adventure rather than allowing your adult mind to be clouded with fear. Be open to the lessons that appear and the healing that might need to occur. Know that you can deal with whatever happens. (And perhaps you will even scream with delight when you achieve your goal!)

Summary

❀ A treasure map can take a variety of forms:

collage	mobile
wreath	let your imagination soar!

Keep your treasure map simple (especially if you tend to procrastinate)

Treasure maps work on the subconscious level

There is no one "right" way to create a treasure map.

❀ A few guidelines:

include a picture of your spiritual source

include a picture of yourself

focus on one goal per treasure map

use the caveat, "This, or something better, is mine now" to eliminate unconscious limits

use color that appeals to you or that represents aspects of your life

include an affirmation and a "thank you" to your spiritual source

keep it private, but view it frequently

❀ Your conscious mind must believe to some degree that the goal on your treasure map is attainable

❀ Once your treasure map is created, issues corresponding to your goal may come up to be healed.

Reflections

Decide on a goal for which you would like to create a treasure map.

_____

_____

_____

_____

_____

_____

_____

_____

_____

_____

_____

_____

_____

_____

_____

_____

_____

_____

_____

_____

_____

Exercise: Creating a Treasure Map

Give yourself the gift of creating a treasure map. Plan on a couple of hours of uninterrupted time when you are feeling calm and unhurried. Gather old magazines, scissors, poster board, glue, or whatever materials you need for the kind of treasure map you wish to create. Invite your inner child out to play, and let yourself have fun with this!

Chapter 7

Step Four: Affirming Your Treasure Map

Our mental commentary influences and colors our feelings and perceptions about what's going on in our lives, and it is these thought forms that ultimately attract and create everything that happens to us.

Shakti Gawain

Imagine that you are going to take a road trip, and you pull out a map to determine your route. But the only thing on the map are lines showing the highways and roads going in various directions—no numbers or words. You might be able to see your destination, but you feel uncertain about your ability to get there. Similarly, a treasure map missing an accompanying affirmation is incomplete. You might know what your goal or destination is, but without an affirmation you are not claiming it as yours; so getting there—if you do—will take much longer. While the affirmation itself does not tell you how to get to your goal, declaring your affirmation on a regular basis brings your goal closer. Declaring your affirmation frequently keeps you open to the opportunities that appear and helps you focus on what you can do to facilitate goal achievement.

An affirmation is a present-tense positive statement that your goal is achieved. Once you have created your treasure map, write on it a specific affirmation about your goal. While this task seems like the simplest part of the process, it is one with which many people have a fair amount of difficulty. You want to believe that your affirmation is true in the present tense (despite appearances to the contrary). You want it to be simple enough to repeat regularly, yet encompassing enough to include all of what your goal represents. There are affirmation examples at the end of this chapter.

It is important that this affirmation not be a rote drill that you rattle off like memorized multiplication facts. The most effective use of affirmations comes when they are declared regularly and with concentration. Say them when you can really picture how you will feel when you have achieved your goal. Say them when you won't be disturbed and you can repeat them out loud. One of my clients liked to sing her affirmations while she worked out on the treadmill. An excellent way to integrate the mind and body!

Speaking of the body, affirmations can be declared for virtually any kind of a goal—including improved physical health. Herbert Benson, M.D., is the founding President of the Mind/Body Medical Institute and is the Mind/Body Medical Institute Associate Professor of Medicine at Harvard Medical School. Author of the well-known *The Relaxation Response* as well as a multitude of other books and articles, he writes: "The mind affects the body; thoughts can alter physiology. Stressful thoughts lead to stressful reactions, while affirmations can lead to positive physiological changes."

Dealing with Uneasy Feelings

Be aware of any gnawing uneasiness that comes up as you state your affirmation. Typically, this is due to a lack of psychological preparation, discussed in chapter 2. If you feel uncomfortable as you declare your affirmation (especially when you say it out loud), try to identify the specific feeling you have—unworthiness, disbelief, guilt, etc. Then, acknowledge the feeling and use one of the releasing exercises at the end of chapter 4 to let it go. Continue to affirm your goal is achieved.

Sometimes, people will feel uneasy about declaring their affirmations because the goal they are affirming is not really theirs. In other words, it is something some-one important to the individual personally desires. If you feel like this might be the case for you, take an internal inventory to be certain your goal is truly your goal. Ask yourself these questions:

> Do you wish to attain this goal because you feel it will impress others?
>
> Is it something you believe others want you to have or be?
>
> What motivated you to name it as a goal?
>
> Is there any element of fear behind your choosing this goal?
>
> Is the motivator some other external factor?

If you discover your goal is externally motivated, it is probably not something your higher self needs or wants, and you will feel uncomfortable claiming it as yours. In addition, you will meet tremendous resistance in achieving it.

The Importance of Internal Integrity

Earlier, you were asked to meditate on the word "pros-perous" in order to write a Personal Prosperity Definition. When you meditate, you are seeking guidance from your highest self. The direction you receive in this manner steers you towards your highest good, so the goals you set are congruent with your innermost desires. This "internal integrity" is absolutely vital to goal achievement. Remember, this process is as much about personal growth and spiritual fulfillment as it is about acquiring things. You take a major step along your path of personal growth when you "own" your goals. That is, they feel totally right to your innermost, highest self, regardless of others' opinions or societal pressures. Then, your treasure map represents something that will promote your highest good—it is in alignment with your values and your authentic self. Certainly, in the process of achieving it, you may have to deal with a few challenges, and the Universe may guide you towards your goal in unexpected ways. In fact, the manifestation of the goal may be somewhat different than you anticipated, but the essence will be the same—or better!

Trust that the Universe will guide you towards your highest good, that it will remind you to get in touch with your internal integrity by re-evaluating your goals, by ascertaining they reflect the desires of your innermost, higher self. When you are comfortable about deserving and believing you can have your goals, and when they truly represent the yearnings of your highest self, affirming them will be a pleasant experience.

Hopelessness to Hopefulness

Probably the most challenging aspect of using affirmations effectively is asserting that your goal is so, when all outer appearances indicate the opposite. Yet that is exactly the time when it is especially important to persevere in affirming your goal. Declaring your affirmations in a positive way provides the power to bring them into manifestation. Conversely, if you get discouraged and quit saying them, or state, "This will never work!" you sabotage your ability to achieve your goals.

The secret to affirming something when you feel hopeless is to think of it in terms of a wonderful mental exercise. Just as physical exercise conditions and tones your body, the exercise of declaring affirmations—even when you have difficulty believing they could ever be "real"—conditions your mind. While physical exercise conditions your body to become more flexible, stronger, and more physically fit, the mental exercise of repeating affirmations conditions your mind to have hope. Many people report that physical exercise helps them feel less depressed. The same is true for affirming your treasure map; affirmations can help lift you from a sense of hopelessness to hopefulness. And just as you sometimes have to force yourself to get physical exercise, you may need to force yourself to say positive affirmations at those times you least feel like it. The wondrous part is that the more you do, the more you will feel like it.

This is why it is important that your treasure map be accessible to you so you can look at it frequently. Repetition is a simple and essential ingredient in the recipe for treasure mapping success. Continuous and persistent effort breaks down resistance. When you repeat a positive affirmation to yourself over and over again—and truly believe it—it will manifest itself. Therein lies one of keys to this process—repetition and belief. Review your map frequently and say its affirmation as often as you can—believing it is true. Then, hold on to your hat, because things are going to start changing!

Where's the Rabbit?

Contrary to some people's wishful thinking, creating a treasure map and saying affirmations is not as magical as declaring "abracadabra" and producing a rabbit from a hat. The psychological preparation, releasing work, present-moment appreciation, and affirmation repetition all require a tremendous amount of mental—and in some cases, emotional—energy, and they need to go on in addition to your everyday life. The good news is that at the same time you are actively "working" the steps, you can release the outcome. In other words, you truly can let go and you don't need to worry about, manipulate, or control the events in your life. Consequently, you experience freedom from the stress and fatigue these controlling behaviors produce. The extent to which you experience this freedom is directly proportional to your ability to trust in the process—and in the Universe to provide—and allow it to work for you. The result is you will experience less stress and fatigue, and you will feel calmer and more serene. So, although there is no rabbit, the transformation in your life as you learn to release, appreciate, affirm, and trust may indeed feel magical.

Summary

❀ An affirmation is a present-tense positive statement that your goal is achieved.

❀ Affirmations help bring your goals closer to manifestation by keeping you open to the opportunities that appear and they help you focus on what you can do to facilitate goal achievement.

❀ Declare your affirmations daily, with concentration, until you attain your goal.

❀ Acknowledge and release uneasy feelings that may come up as you state your affirmations.

❀ Be certain you "own" your goals.

❀ It is especially important to use affirmations when outer appearances seem to be to the contrary.

❀ One way to sabotage your goal achievement is to quit declaring your affirmations.

❀ Declaring affirmations is a mental exercise that conditions the mind to receive.

❀ You can let go of controlling behaviors when you treasure map and begin declaring affirmations.

Reflections: Affirmations

The affirmation you write on your treasure map will be specific to your goal. The following suggestions will get you started, although it is more effective to create your own affirmations. In this way, you are forced to really think about what it is you are claiming; a greater sense of ownership and responsibility are created. Be as specific as possible.

"The right and perfect job is mine, now."

"I am in a job that I find fulfilling, challenging, and financially rewarding."

"My work environment is positive and supportive, and I enjoy a mutually respectful, harmonious relationship with all the people with whom I work."

"My right and perfect partner is mine, now."

"I am healthy, energetic, slender and strong!"

"I am calm and confident in all that I think, say, and do."

Use this page to write your own affirmations.

_____

_____

_____

_____

_____

_____

_____

_____

_____

_____

_____

_____

_____

_____

_____

_____

_____

_____

_____

_____

_____

_____

Chapter 8

Step Five: Receiving

It is a funny thing about life;
if you refuse to accept anything but the best,
you very often get it.

W. Somerset Maugham

One Christmas, when my daughter was very young, she received a gift that thrilled her so much she actually squealed when she opened it. The remarkable part about this was not that the gift was so fantastic, but that she received it so openly and joyfully. So often, as in this instance, it is young children that teach important lessons. Learning to receive openly, joyfully, and gratefully is a key ingredient in successful treasure mapping.

Yet, receiving in treasure mapping is more challenging than simply opening a gift-wrapped package and discovering a wonderful surprise. Before you "receive" your goal, you will also need to be open to receiving the more subtle gifts the Universe will provide towards goal manifestation. These gifts will take a variety of forms: You may receive inspiration from a book, speaker, or counselor about what you could do to achieve your goals. You may receive information about a group or organization you could join that might be helpful as you pursue what you want to do. You might meet someone who gives you just the advice you need to guide you toward accomplishing your goals. You may simply act on a notion that "comes to you," a notion that somehow facilitates manifestation of your goals. In short, instead of receiving *things,* you may receive inspiration, information, advice, opportunities, or even feelings that will guide you towards your goal manifestation. In order for your treasure map to be successful, it is vital that you stay open to receive, and act on, these signals.

Resistance to Receive

Although it would seem that receiving would be the easiest of all the treasure mapping steps, it is actually one where people are very likely to sabotage themselves. This seems to happen either because they don't recognize the gift when it appears, and they snub it; or they realize that it is related to their goal but are unwilling to take the action required.

It reminds me of the story of the priest who defied the warnings to leave town because a dangerous storm was approaching. The priest confidently stated, "I won't worry, God will save me." The morning of the storm, the police went through the neighborhood telling everyone to evacuate. The priest stood his ground, replying, "I won't worry, God will save me." The storm drains backed up and there were several inches of water in the street. A fire truck went to pick up the priest, who again refused the help, telling them, "Don't worry, God will save me." The water continued to rise. The National Guard sent a boat to rescue him, but the priest stubbornly repeated what he told the others, "Don't worry, God will save me." The water rose enough that he was forced up to the roof. A helicopter flew in to pick him up, but he shouted up at them, "Don't worry, God will save me." But alas, he fell from the roof into the swirling water and drowned. When he got to heaven, he told God, "I've been your faithful servant ever since I was born! Why didn't you save me?" God replied, "First, I sent the police, then a fire truck, then the National Guard, and even a helicopter. What more do you want from me!!??"

Just as the priest didn't recognize that the police, firemen, National Guard, and helicopter were in fact, "God with skin on," we sometimes miss the opportunities that come our way because we simply don't recognize them as the gifts that they are, or we refuse to accept them and consequently, sabotage ourselves. In either case, I suspect there is a fair amount of resistance to change. When things don't change, or the treasure map doesn't "work," we wonder why.

In my career counseling practice, I frequently meet folks who are masters at sabotaging themselves. I call them the "Yes-buts." Although they have made the effort to see a career counselor, usually because they are unhappy in their jobs, they resist the suggestions I make about things they could do to improve their situations with reasons why they think it won't work. "Yes, but, I'm too old"; "Yes, but, I've tried that"; "Yes, but, what if...?" Steven Pressfield, author of *The War of Art* is adamant about the role resistance plays in keeping us unfulfilled. He writes:

"Resistance is the most toxic force on the planet. It is the root of more unhappiness than poverty, disease, and erectile dysfunction. To yield to Resistance deforms our spirit. It stunts us and makes us less than we are and were born to be. . . ."

Strong words? Perhaps, but whether you are resisting suggestions related to your job search, or refusing the gifts the Universe offers, you are probably sabotaging your ability to maximize your potential and be all you were born to be.

Tuning In

Sometimes, the messages the Universe sends us seem like annoying static on a radio that it isn't quite tuned to the right station. We know there is something there, but it's not very clear. It is very helpful, once your treasure map is created, to practice "tuning in" to the messages coming your way. You can do this by meditating on a daily basis, or as mentioned earlier, by remembering to get silent and to listen. As you practice tuning in and listening, you enhance your intuitive ability. Soon, those messages of inspiration, information, opportunities, and advice will be very clear. Acting on them will become second nature to you.

This worked for me when I first made a treasure map about writing this book. Before I had even started writing it, I meditated on how to proceed. I "received" the idea to first write query letters to publishers and agencies to get a sense of the interest in this topic. On a rational level, it seemed like a discouraging idea. After all, my research about submitting query letters indicated that responses—if I got any—would take months. Nevertheless, because I was practicing trusting my intuition, I did more research and selected four publishers and one agency to which I sent my query. Imagine my surprise, when within one month after sending my queries, I had a response from all five! Although three of them were not interested, it seemed to me that getting all five responses to my query so quickly was a positive signal. This motivated me to start writing. If I had had the idea to write query letters and chosen not to do anything about it, this book might still be just an idea floating around in my head.

The point is, when you care enough about a particular goal to treasure map for it, be certain you are not only willing to be aware of the messages you receive, but be willing to take the action steps necessary to reach that goal. You are an active participant in this process, and the more willing you are to receive the opportunities that come up for you, and the more you really listen to your intuition, the sooner you will achieve results.

You Will Get What You Intend, Maybe Not What You Expect

The Rolling Stones had a popular song that included the lyrics:

> You can't always get what you want
> But if you try ... you might find
> You get what you need.

Sometimes the results of treasure mapping are like the song lyrics. Your route to your goal might take some unusual turns, and while you may not get exactly what you thought you wanted, you will likely get what you intended. The experiences of two clients might explain this more clearly. Laurie was a computer consultant who attended one of my first treasure mapping workshops. Laurie found she was doing more computer programming than consulting, which frustrated her, because she wanted to work more directly with people. At the workshop, she created a treasure map with "consulting" as the theme. Within two weeks she was presented with a consulting opportunity—but it had nothing to do with computers. Nevertheless, she was open to the possibilities the new opportunity provided and willing to take the necessary steps to give it a try. Before long, Laurie had established a lucrative second income for herself as a cosmetics consultant! Not only was it financially rewarding, she also got to work with many different people in a more creative way than she had ever imagined. In fact, she was so successful that within her first twelve months she won a trip to the Bahamas. Her ability to be open to the possible routes her path could take—to receive and to act on the messages she was getting—enabled her to get results she might never have thought of had she used traditional goal setting, focusing only on computer consulting.

Another client was a high school girl who created a treasure map with a goal of being on her school's homecoming court. As it turned out, she was not selected to be on court. Before I could say anything, she explained it had turned out better than she expected. She confessed that her true intention in wanting to run for court had been to increase her confidence and to meet a particular young man. She told me she gained a lot of confidence conducting her campaign running for homecoming court. But even better, the young man in whom she was interested was also running for court and did not get elected either. He invited her to go to the homecoming activities with him, which of course she did. This was not what she expected when she made her map, but exactly what she intended!

Receiving Your Goal

Clearly, a huge factor in successful treasure mapping is willingness to receive—both the messages the Universe provides and the manifestation of the goal itself. Ronae, who also attended one of my first workshops, demonstrated that willingness to receive. Six days after the workshop, she wrote me this letter:

> Dear Barb,
> You said you wanted to know the results of our treasure maps, so here's mine.
>
> It was so quick I am almost scared to do another one.
>
> May 13—I went to the Treasure Mapping workshop. I had decided to Treasure Map for a car

but had no preference for one kind or another. I found a picture of a Dodge Daytona and pasted it on my green paper.

May 14—After having thought more about Treasure Mapping, I went and got paper and magazines and put a Hyundai with specific options on a new piece of green paper. I put on my affirmation and hung it up so I would see it often. (I left the "old" map face down in a chair.)

May 15—[I accidentally dump my car keys in the garbage. Guess I'm ready to release my old car?]

May 16—On my way home . . . I passed a car dealership and wondered if I should start visiting them to find my car. I decided that if the Universe had a car for me "It" would be there. . . . I turned the corner and there "It" was!! A Dodge Colt—a Dodge like the map from the workshop but in the shape of a Hyundai like the second map!

May 17—I called the number on the car—it had all the options I listed on my map . . .

May 18—We transferred the title of the car—it's mine!!

Within five days after creating a treasure map for a different car, she had one! Although initially Ronae was not particular about the model, after thinking about it a little more, she got much more intentional and specific about what she wanted. She was willing to receive and act on the message to turn at the corner by car dealership, listening to her intuition that the car would be "there." "There" turned out to be in front of a house next to the dealership, but had she not been paying attention to the message she was getting, she might have missed her opportunity. From a logical point of view, she was expecting it would be several months before she was able to purchase a different car; she could never have predicted that it would happen so quickly. Not everyone will experience results in such a short time frame, but it certainly is possible when you are intentional, specific, and willing to receive.

It is interesting to note that by her own admission, the speed of this success made Ronae almost scared to make another treasure map. Thinking of success as "frightening" can block further good from manifesting. If you are concerned that prompt results will alarm you, it is helpful to affirm on your treasure map: "I am ready to receive now," or "I accept my good now." You may want to start by giving yourself permission to receive. Another way to prepare to receive is simply to practice receiving. One very simple way to do this is just to say "thank you" when someone gives you a compliment. Then, do something for yourself that you consider a "guilty pleasure" (getting a massage, reading a book in the middle of the day, letting a companion treat you to dinner). As you become more comfortable with receiving, you will be less likely to sabotage the good that comes your way and far more likely to achieve your goals.

It may be that you won't squeal with delight when you accomplish your goals. But when you are ready and willing to receive them in childlike fashion, openly and joyfully, you will be on your way to personal and professional fulfillment. Your Dream-Seeker will be re-awakened!

Summary

✽ Learning to receive openly and joyfully is a key ingredient in successful treasure mapping.

✽ Gifts you may need to learn to receive before you accomplish your goal include:
> inspiration
> information
> opportunities
> advice
> feelings

✽ Resistance to our gifts inhibits our ability to maximize our potential.

✽ Tune in to the messages through meditation, silence and listening.

✽ The manifestation of your goal may be different than you expect.

✽ Practice receiving.

Reflections: Receiving Exercise

Some things I would like to do to practice receiving:
[Idea starters: Saying "Thank you" when you are given
a compliment; reading a book in the middle of the day;
getting a massage; taking a bubble bath; allowing a
friend to buy you coffee.]

_____

_____

_____

_____

_____

_____

_____

_____

_____

_____

_____

_____

_____

_____

_____

_____

_____

Resources

Gawain, Shakti. *Creative Visualization*. Nataraj
    Publishing: Novato, CA, 2002.

Hay, Louise, L. *You Can Heal Your Life*. Hay House:
    Santa Monica, CA, 1984.

Hyder, Carole J.. *Wind and Water: Your Personal Feng
    Shui Journey*. Crossing Press: Freedom, CA, 2001.

Kingston, Karen. *Clear Your Clutter with Feng Shui*.
    Broadway Books: New York, 1999.

Leider, Richard and David Shapiro. *Repacking Your
    Bags*. Berrett-Koehler Publishers, San Francisco,
    1996.

Ponder, Catherine. *Open Your Mind to Receive*. DeVorss
    & Company: Marina del Ray, CA, 1983.

Ponder, Catherine. *The Dynamic Laws of Prosperity*.
    DeVorss & Company: Marina del Ray, CA, 1985.

Pressfield, Steven. *The War of Art: Break Through the
    Blocks and Win Your Inner Creative Battles*. Warner
    Books: [city], 2002.

Robbins, Anthony. *Unlimited Power*. Simon & Schuster,
    New York: 1986.

Rogers, Fred. *The World According to Mister Rogers
    {Important Things to Remember}*. Hyperion: New
    York, 2003.

Williamson, Marianne. *A Return to Love*.
    HarperCollins: New York, 1992.

Zukav, Gary and Linda Francis. *The Mind of the Soul*.
    Simon & Schuster: New York, 2003.

About the Author

Barbara Laporte's expertise in helping clients manage career and life transitions comes not just from her educational training in which she earned a Master's degree in Human Development, or her twenty-plus years of professional experience in employee training and career counseling.

Equally important in shaping her ability to touch readers and clients with compassion and insight are the significant transitions and multiple losses she has experienced in her own life.

Since she discovered treasure mapping as a goal accomplishment technique in the 1980s, Barbara has used, refined, and taught this powerful tool with remarkable success. Some of the goals that have been achieved using treasure maps include:

Weddings
Real estate transactions
Weight loss
Successful job transitions
Improved health
Work / life balance

Barb and her husband, Ron Lewandowski, live in New Brighton, Minnesota.